Discovering
London Ceremonial
and Traditions

Julian Paget

Shire Publications

British Library Cataloguing in Publication Data: Paget, Julian. Discovering London ceremonial and traditions. – 2nd ed. 1. Processions – England – London 2. Great Britain – Kings and rulers I. Title II. London ceremonial and traditions 394.5'09421 ISBN 0 7478 0408 7.

Acknowledgements
Photographs are acknowledged as follows: from the Royal Archives, reproduced by gracious permission of Her Majesty The Queen, pages 18, 62; reproduced by kind permission of the Headquarters of the Household Division, pages 8 (bottom), 13, 28, 36, 39, 43, 46, 48, 86; Cadbury Lamb, pages 8 (top), 10 (both), 15, 21, 22, 23, 25, 29, 30, 31, 32, 33, 35, 45, 49 (both), 52 (both), 53, 54, 57, 58, 60, 61, 65, 69, 70 (both), 72, 73, 74, 75, 78, 79, 83, 84, 85, 89, 90, 91, 96; Sir Julian Paget, pages 6, 16, 19, 27, 34, 38, 42 (both), 44, 59; Sue Ross, page 66. The photograph on page 80 is from an old postcard. The map is by D. R. Darton.

Printed in Malta By Gutenberg Press Limited, Gudja Road, Tarxien PLA19, Malta.

Contents

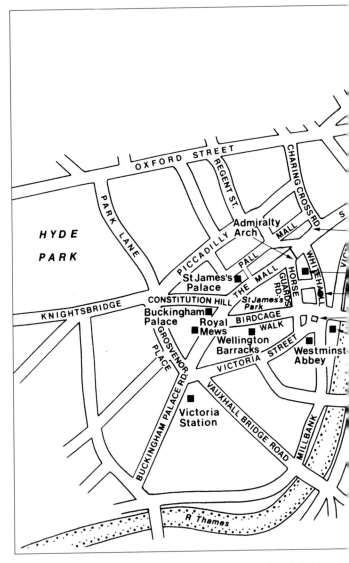

Map of central London showing the principal places mentioned in the book.

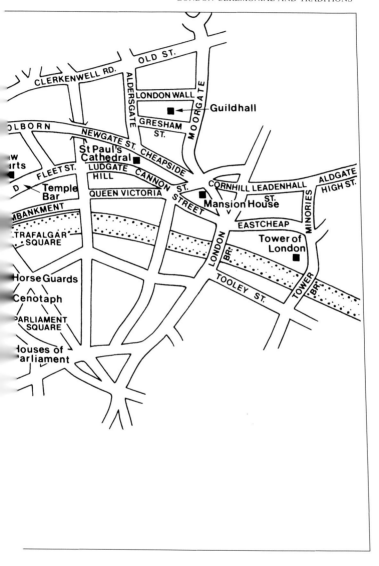

The Queen's Birthday Parade: the Guards march past.

1. Introduction

London has a wonderful, rich tapestry of ceremonial that is unique in the world, and unsurpassed. It is no mere display or entertainment but reflects centuries of history and tradition.

It has always centred round the Monarchy, dating back to medieval times, when the King was the actual ruler of the country, and his household was in effect the government of the day. He had to impress the turbulent, ambitious nobles with his power, and at the same time he wanted to present a 'right royal image' to his subjects. He also needed good protection at all times, either mounted escorts in battle or guards on his royal palaces, and so, until the nineteenth century, the Household Troops and the Royal Bodyguards provided this protection continuously; but now there is no such role for them, and their duties are largely ceremonial.

There are several reasons why this ceremonial is so special, and why it has survived. First, there is a reason for every aspect of it, which gives it meaning. For example, the Household Cavalry Escort to The Queen on a State occasion is carrying out virtually the same role as it has done since 1660, and it is as important today as it was then.

Second, ceremonial has evolved through the ages and has always adapted to changing times. Those responsible for organising great State occasions are well aware of the problems, such as trying to reconcile ancient traditions with modern traffic. Some events have been abandoned, and others (including Trooping the Colour and the Lord Mayor's Show) have been changed from weekdays to Saturdays, so as to interfere less with London's traffic. Rehearsals often take place at dawn, long before commuters are on the streets, and every effort is made to prevent the ceremonial becoming either a nuisance or an anachronism.

The troops who take part in ceremonial are primarily still fighting men who can switch from tunic and bearskin to combat clothing at any time. Indeed, in 1982, the Scots and Welsh Guards changed from practising for The Queen's Birthday Parade to prepare for war and were fighting three months later in the Falklands.

London's ceremonial is not just a matter for those who take part, for those who watch are also involved – the cheerful spectators who sit through a chilly night to be in the front row next morning, and those who cheer and wave and explain it all to the children. Without them, it would all have little meaning or purpose and it is hoped that this book will increase their understanding and enjoyment.

One of the Windsor Greys with State harness, being ridden by a Postillion wearing Full State Livery.

The Royal Procession crossing Horse Guards Parade on the way to Westminster.

2. Discovering London Ceremonial

London's ceremonial consists of a number of events that can be seen and enjoyed by everyone. A few, such as the Changing of the Guard at Buckingham Palace and at Horse Guards, take place every day. Most of them occur annually on dates that vary each year. These events fall into two categories: the royal ceremonial, in which the Sovereign is involved, directly or indirectly, and the ceremonial of the City of London, which is a separate entity with its own unique customs and traditions.

The Royal Route

Whenever the Sovereign sets out from Buckingham Palace on a State occasion, the Royal Procession follows a long-established route that has changed little since the late seventeenth century. From 1698 the Court was at St James's Palace, and the Sovereign would travel to Westminster across the Horse Guards parade ground, through the Arch into Whitehall and so to Parliament Square. Today the only difference is that the Procession starts from Buckingham Palace and follows that impressive ceremonial approach, The Mall, which was created in 1912.

The whole length of the Royal Route is normally lined by troops of the Armed Forces, carrying out a duty that dates back to the seventeenth century. There was no police force in London until 1827, and before that the Royal Route had to be kept open and protected by troops, a custom that is continued today. Nor is their function purely ceremonial, for when a youth fired a blank pistol at The Queen in The Mall in 1981 it was a Scots Guards corporal on street-lining duty who was the first to seize him.

When The Queen visits the City of London for any State occasion, her route runs down The Mall, through Admiralty Arch and then along the Strand to the City boundary at Temple Bar in Fleet Street. There she is met by the Lord Mayor, who then precedes Her Majesty while she is within the City. There is a simple but symbolic ceremony at Temple Bar, which is described in chapter 17.

Places to visit

Most of the places connected with London's ceremonial are to be found along the Royal Route and are situated in such a way that they may conveniently be visited in the course of two circuits. The first is centred on St James's Park and includes eight places, which can be visited in the following order: 1, Buckingham Palace; 2, the Royal

St James's Palace.

Mews; 3, Wellington Barracks; 4, St James's Palace; 5, Horse Guards; 6, Whitehall; 7, Westminster Abbey; 8, The Palace of Westminster.

The second circuit covers places connected with City of London ceremonial, which are: 1, Temple Bar; 2, St Paul's Cathedral; 3, Guildhall.

Last, but very important, there is the Tower of London, which is a Royal Palace and Fortress and is therefore associated with royal ceremonial. It is located by Tower Bridge next to the City of London, although not actually within its boundaries.

Guards line Horse Guards awaiting The Queen's coach.

3. The People Involved

The people who plan and take part in the many ceremonial events that we all enjoy watching cover a wide range of occupations, titles and trades; they range from the police constable on duty in The Mall to the Lord High Constable in his peer's robes in Westminster Abbey. Many thousands of people are involved in each event, which is not unlike a huge theatre production, with London as the stage on which the ceremonial is presented for an audience which may, through television, amount to over 500 million worldwide.

The planners

It is a complex undertaking to arrange an elaborate State occasion such as a Royal Wedding, which it is possible to plan many months ahead. Even more difficult is a Royal Funeral, for the timing cannot be foreseen; it was a considerable achievement to arrange Earl Mountbatten's impressive funeral within a mere six days of his death. There is usually a degree of contingency planning, and this was done, for example, for the funeral of Queen Elizabeth The Queen Mother in 2002, and also for Sir Winston Churchill's State Funeral in 1965, when an outline plan was worked out years ahead with the code name 'Operation Hope Not'.

Responsibility for organising all ceremonial in England and Wales rests with two officers, the Earl Marshal and the Lord Chamberlain; each deals with a separate aspect, and this has led to them being described on occasions as 'the rival impresarios'.

The **Earl Marshal of England** is responsible for all State Ceremonial, that is those events that are national in character. These include the Coronation and the funeral (but not the wedding) of the Sovereign; State Funerals, such as that of Sir Winston Churchill in 1965; the Investiture of the Prince of Wales, which takes place at Caernarfon Castle; and also the State Opening of Parliament. He has no authority in Scotland, where ceremonial is organised by Lord Lyon, King of Arms.

The appointment of Earl Marshal dates back to medieval times, and he is the only one of the seven Great Officers of State whose ceremonial post is still active and full-time. (The others, in order of precedence, are the Lord High Steward, the Lord Chancellor, the Lord President of the Council, the Lord Privy Seal, the Lord Great Chamberlain and the Lord High Constable.) He is *ex officio* Head of the College of Arms, the headquarters of the Heralds, and they help him with his planning and organisation. The title has since 1672 been hereditary to the Howard family, the Dukes of Norfolk, and with it goes a salary of just £20 *per annum*, this being the rate agreed by King Richard III in 1483 and never changed since.

The other impresario is the **Lord Chamberlain**, who is broadly responsible for all Royal as opposed to State ceremonial. He is Head of the Royal Household and therefore organises events involving the Royal Family that are not in the domain of the Earl Marshal. These include Royal Weddings, Royal Funerals (other than the Sovereign's), Investitures, Jubilee celebrations and State Visits. His duties are many and remarkably diverse, ranging from custody of the Crown Jewels (a task retained from Anglo-Saxon times) and advising on appointments such as those of the Poet Laureate and the Queen's Bargemaster, to the issue of a thousand or so Royal Warrants and the care of the royal swans on the river Thames.

With the help of a remarkably small staff, he controls the complex planning and precise timing of most ceremonial occasions in London, knowing exactly how many seconds to allow for each handshake and for every yard covered, be it on foot, by car, by carriage or by launch. He also co-ordinates and orchestrates the many different bodies involved, such as the Royal Bodyguards, the Armed Forces, the Police, the press and television (through the Queen's Press Secretary), local authorities and local dignitaries, as well as similar organisations from other countries.

The Lord Chamberlain takes part in most royal ceremonial events, but traditionally he does not attend the State Opening of Parliament. On that occasion he is deliberately left behind and is placed in charge of the security of Buckingham Palace, to safeguard it against a coup in the absence of the Sovereign. This was a wise precaution in medieval times, and the custom has been retained.

The dividing line between the duties of the Lord Chamberlain and those of the Earl Marshal is narrow and subtle, but the arrangement works well and their expertise ensures the standards of perfection that we have come to take for granted.

It was not always so, and the organisation in the nineteenth century was decidedly haphazard. Queen Victoria was late for her own Coronation, and the service nearly ended prematurely because the Bishop of Bath and Wells turned over two pages by mistake and led the Queen away into a side chapel, where they were met by the Dean, who sent them back to complete the missing page.

An incident occurred at Queen Victoria's funeral which was to become a firm tradition. The gun carriage bearing the royal coffin had been drawn through London without incident, and the cortege assembled at Windsor on 2nd February 1901 to await the royal coffin, which was to follow from London by train. The gun carriage was to be drawn by horses of the Royal Horse Artillery, but it was a chilly morning and one of the horses became restless, lashed out and broke its traces. The damage could not be repaired on the spot, and there was a major problem of how to get the coffin up the hill to St George's Chapel.

The crisis was solved by one of the Queen's Naval aides-de-camp, who suggested that the Royal Navy Guard of Honour, a hundred strong, should take over. So, using the harness of the horses, supplemented by the communication cord of the Royal Train, the sailors took the place of the horses and the procession continued on its way. Having saved the day on that occasion, naval ratings have drawn the gun carriage at Royal and State Funerals ever since. In such ways are traditions created.

The Guards

A major contribution to London's ceremonial comes from the Household Troops, better known as 'The Guards'. They consist of two regiments of **Household Cavalry** (The Life Guards, and The Blues and Royals) and five regiments of **Foot Guards** (in order of seniority: the Grenadier Guards, Coldstream Guards, Scots Guards, Irish Guards, and Welsh Guards). They have been the personal troops of the

The Queen's Life Guard mounts daily at Horse Guards regardless of the weather.

13

Sovereign since the seventeenth century, except for the Irish Guards, who were formed in 1900, and the Welsh Guards, who were created in 1915. Although their ceremonial duties are such a tourist attraction, this is not their main role, for they are primarily operational troops in peace as well as war.

The Household Cavalry consists of one operational armoured regiment called the Household Cavalry Regiment; the ceremonial role is carried out by officers and men who are serving temporarily with a purely ceremonial unit called the Household Cavalry Mounted Regiment, in London. They abandon their tanks for two to three years and in many cases have to learn to ride in ceremonial dress, which is no easy task.

The Foot Guards do not have any one unit specialising in ceremonial but expect all battalions to carry out both roles, doing a three-year tour in London in between operational postings. As a result, they have taken part in virtually every campaign in which the British Army has participated since 1945, and more than half of them are normally stationed overseas.

The two Household Cavalry regiments are easily distinguished on parade, because The Life Guards wear scarlet tunics and white plumes on their helmets, while The Blues and Royals have blue tunics with red plumes. The trumpeters of both regiments wear red plumes and are mounted, as ordered by King James II, on grey rather than black horses, so that they were easily distinguishable in battle when required to sound a call.

The Foot Guards may at first sight look alike in their tunics and bearskins, but it is possible to identify them by three features: the plume on the bearskins, the spacing of the buttons on the tunics, and the regimental badges on the collar and shoulder of the tunics. These points are best tabulated:

Regiment	Plume	Buttons	Collar badge	Shoulder badge
Grenadier Guards	White, worn on the left	Singly	Grenade	Royal Cipher
Coldstream Guards	Red, worn on the right	Pairs	Garter Star	Rose
Scots Guards	None	Threes	Thistle Star	Thistle
Irish Guards	Blue, worn on the right	Fours	Shamrock	Star of the Order of St Patrick
Welsh Guards	White-green-white, worn on the left	Fives	Leek	Leek

A Household Cavalry skewbald drum horse, with the solid silver drum.

Bands

No ceremonial is complete without martial music, and the Guards Bands play a major part, together with those of all three Services.

The Household Cavalry have two unique mounted bands, led by their famous skewbald drum horses, carrying the solid silver kettle drums presented by the Sovereign. George III presented two to The Blues in 1805, and William IV gave two to The Life Guards in 1831. The musicians wear a magnificent State Dress of gold and scarlet, like the State Trumpeters, who sound fanfares on so many royal occasions. They control their mounts by reins attached to their ankles or to the wrists that are playing instruments, so they have to be highly trained horsemen as well as skilled musicians.

No one can fail to be moved by the sight and sound of the Massed Bands and Pipes and Drums of the Guards on parade, four hundred strong and marching as one, on The Queen's Birthday Parade or Beating Retreat. The drill is as impressive as the music, and their special manoeuvre, the 'spin wheel', is so complicated that the finer points have never been written down, but are passed on by word of mouth from one Director of Music to another.

Music is an important part of all ceremonial, ranging from rousing marches and the skirl of the pipes to the notes of 'Last Post' at sunset and the echoing organ music in abbey or cathedral.

The Heralds

The Heralds in their splendid scarlet, blue and gold tabards, which make them look like the Knave of Hearts, are very much a part of London's ceremonial. With their black velvet caps, black breeches and white stockings, they add much to the colour of the occasion.

They date back to the thirteenth century, when the Monarch and most nobles retained heralds as organisers, announcers and scorers at the great tournaments that were popular then. To do this, the heralds had to be able to identify knights in armour by the arms on their shields, and so they soon became experts on heraldry and genealogical matters. A gathering of armed barons and knights at a tournament posed a potential risk to the security of the Sovereign in those turbulent days, and a set of rules for these tournaments written

Heralds in their tabards.

16

in 1267 decreed that 'Kings of Heralds might carry no concealed weapons save their blunted swords' and also that 'no groom or footman might carry a pointed sword, pointed knife, club, stick or stone on pain of lying seven years in gaol'.

The chief Herald is Garter, King of Arms, who is supported by Clarence, King of Arms, responsible for the area south of the river Trent, and Norroy and Ulster, who controls north of the Trent (but not Scotland, which has its own Heralds). In addition to the three Kings of Arms, there are six Heralds, bearing the titles of Windsor, Richmond, Somerset, Lancaster, York and Chester – designations acquired in the middle of the fourteenth century from the lordships, castles or arms of their masters. In the fifteenth century, some junior or probationary heralds were also appointed, called Pursuivants (pronounced 'persevant'). Four survive today, bearing the mysterious titles of Rouge Croix (the Cross of St George), Blue Mantle (the Mantle of the Garter), Rouge Dragon (the Dragon of Wales), and Portcullis (the badge of the Somerset and Beaufort family, from which Henry VII was descended).

One of the duties of the Heralds is to make the official Proclamation of the Accession of a new Sovereign. It is made first from the balcony of St James's Palace by Garter, King of Arms, in the presence of the Earl Marshal. Garter then drives in a carriage procession with an escort from the Household Cavalry and repeats the Proclamation at Charing Cross, because this was once regarded as the centre of London. Finally, he enters the City of London and reads his Proclamation twice more, once at Chancery Lane and once at the Royal Exchange.

Royal Bodyguards

Throughout the ages most rulers have had their personal bodyguards to protect them in peace and war. In Britain there was no police force until 1827, and the Sovereign has since Tudor times had two Royal Bodyguards in England, the Yeomen of the Guard and the Gentlemen at Arms. Originally they were responsible for guarding the Monarch and his palaces all the time, but now their role has become purely ceremonial and they appear only on State occasions. (Scotland has its own Royal Bodyguard, the Royal Company of Archers.)

The **Yeomen of the Guard** are the oldest Royal Bodyguard in the world, having been formed in 1485 by King Henry VII when he came to the throne after the battle of Bosworth. At his Coronation on 31st October 1485 he declared that his Yeomen were not only for his personal protection but also for 'the upholding of the dignity and grandeur of the English Crown, in perpetuity, his successors, the

A group of Yeomen of the Guard in their Tudor uniform.

Kings and Queens of England, for all times'. His instructions are still faithfully carried out.

There are six officers and eighty-one Yeomen in the Bodyguard, and they are all retired members of the Army, Royal Marines or Royal Air Force. Between them they have well over five hundred campaign medals and awards for gallantry.

Their magnificent scarlet uniform dates back to Tudor times, and the history of the English monarchy is woven into the gold-embroidered emblems on the front and back. There one can see the Tudor crown, with the York and Lancaster roses superimposed below it. The Stuarts added the motto *Dieu et mon droit*, while Queen Anne added the thistle in 1709, following the Union of England and Scotland. When Ireland joined the Union in 1801 George III added the shamrock. The initials of the reigning Monarch appear on either side of the motto, and five centuries of history are thus on display.

Today the Yeomen are on duty part-time only, appearing when summoned for some eight to ten occasions a year. They are in attendance at the Coronation, Lying-in-State and Funeral of the Sovereign, the Investiture of the Prince of Wales at Caernarfon Castle, all Investitures and Garden Parties at Buckingham Palace, and the Royal Maundy Service, where they play a leading part.

The Yeomen of the Guard are often confused with the Yeoman Warders at the Tower of London, but they are two quite distinct bodies with very different duties, although they wear almost identical Tudor

A Yeoman Warder at the Tower of London in State dress.

uniforms. The Yeomen of the Guard are, as we have seen, a Royal Bodyguard, whereas the Yeoman Warders live and work within the Tower, looking after the fortress and its contents. Much of the confusion may be attributed to Gilbert and Sullivan, for when they wrote their famous operetta about the Yeoman Warders at the Tower in 1887 they gave it the misleading title of *The Yeomen of the Guard*.

There is one clear-cut difference in their uniforms: the Yeomen of the Guard wear a gold cross-belt over their left shoulder, but the Yeoman Warders do not. It was originally used in the sixteenth century to carry the weapon with which a Yeoman of the Guard went to battle with the King; the Yeoman Warders never did this.

The other Royal Bodyguard to be seen on ceremonial occasions in London is the **Honourable Corps of Gentlemen at Arms**. Their distinctive uniform is similar to that of an officer of the Dragoon Guards in the 1840s. It has a skirted red coat, embroidered with the Tudor royal badge of the Portcullis, which is the badge also of the Corps. Their helmets with long white feathers are worn at all times when on duty, even in church. Swords are worn, and the Gentlemen also carry long ceremonial 'battle axes', some of which are thought to be over three hundred years old.

The Corps today consists of five officers and twenty-seven Gentlemen; the honorary appointment of Captain is always held by the Government Chief Whip in the House of Lords, which led to the strange situation that from 1974 to 1979 the Captain of the Gentlemen at Arms was a lady, the Baroness Llewelyn-Davies of Hastoe.

All members of the Corps are retired officers from the Army or the Royal Marines, and until the nineteenth century appointments to it used to be purchased and transferred for substantial sums. The post of Lieutenant, for example, was valued in 1783 at about £6000 (a considerable sum in those days), while a Gentleman could obtain a thousand guineas for his position.

As officers, the Gentlemen take precedence over the Yeomen of the Guard, although the latter were formed twenty-four years earlier. The Gentlemen also hold the coveted title of 'The Nearest Guard', which means that they have the privilege of standing nearest to the Sovereign on State occasions. At a Coronation they have the special duty of being 'On Guard' at Westminster Abbey, and at the Sovereign's Funeral they are traditionally among those entitled to be 'On Watch' at the Lying-in-State in Westminster Hall (see chapter 26). They also escort the coffin in the Funeral Procession, as well as being on duty in St George's Chapel, Windsor, for the service there.

The Gentlemen at Arms were created by Henry VIII in 1509 as his 'new and sumptuous Troop of Gentlemen', a title probably inspired by the French court, where the royal guard was called *Gentilhommes de l'Hotel du Roy ou Pensionnaires*. Indeed, they were until 1834 known as the 'Band of Gentlemen Pensioners', the word 'Pensioner' meaning someone who ate at the King's table, rather than a person drawing a pension like the Chelsea Pensioners.

Their original role was to provide a mounted escort for the Sovereign in peace and war, but from about 1526 they began doing duty on foot as well. They have not acted as a Royal Bodyguard in battle since the Civil War of 1642–9 but have twice been called upon to defend the Sovereign in peacetime. In 1553 they prepared to protect Queen Mary during Sir Thomas Wyatt's rebellion, while some three hundred years later they were summoned by Royal Command to defend St James's Palace against possible attack during the Chartist riots in 1848. Perhaps rather to their regret, they did not in the end have to go into action.

The Police

The Metropolitan Police and the City of London Police can justifiably be described as protectors of London's ceremonial, for without them virtually none of it would take place. Yet their contribution is seldom recognised or appreciated. We take it for granted that each occasion will pass off without incident, but this is achieved only by a massive and most efficient effort on the part of the Police.

Crowd control is not the major problem, and there were only some 2300 police on duty for the Golden Jubilee Procession in 2002.

The unwelcome new responsibility for the Police is the increased security risk at all ceremonial events. The policemen on duty can no longer watch proceedings but must turn their backs on their Queen in order to watch the crowds and guard against terrorists. In addition, every building and vantage point along the Royal Route must be checked and controlled to prevent a disaster such as struck President Kennedy in Dallas in 1963.

But, despite the security problem, the Police are still able to take part in London's ceremonial. Their Mounted Branch customarily provides a Royal Escort for most carriage processions, with five horses leading and four behind. In 1977 they also found a mounted Escort for The Queen on her return from the City on 7th June. Other

Mounted police on duty at Westminster.

duties for them are escorting Royal Guards through London's traffic each day and also providing reliable horses for others to ride; many a high-ranking public figure, unskilled as a horseman but obliged to appear mounted on some ceremonial occasion, has had cause to be grateful to the Police for providing a quiet, reliable horse.

The Mounted Branch is probably the oldest section of the Metropolitan Police Force, 'two pursuit horses and proper pursuers' having been appointed to help the peace officers in the capital as early as 1756, seventy-one years before the first police officers appeared on the streets. From 1805 the Bow Street Horse Patrol began doing duty on all main roads up to 20 miles (32 km) from Charing Cross, and the Mounted Police have flourished ever since.

Mounted police escort the royal carriage procession into Whitehall.

4. The City of London

The City of London has a thousand years of tradition behind it, and from this springs its own special ceremonial, which is carefully maintained, even in the twenty-first century. Nowhere else in the world can one see the chairmen of banks, stockbrokers and international financiers walking in solemn procession, carrying nosegays, or even dressed in armour as seventeenth-century pikemen. But it happens in London and shows that ancient and modern can be happily blended.

The City is a remarkable place. It is a mere 677 acres (274 hectares), slightly more than the 'Square Mile', which it is sometimes called. The resident population is under 10,000, but this swells to over 350,000 during office hours. It has its own parliament (the Court of Common Council), its own Corporation and its own police force. It encompasses St Paul's Cathedral, the Mansion House, Guildhall and the Bank of England, but not the Tower of London, which was excluded in the seventeenth century. It has its own Lord Mayor with his own State Coach, and also a number of traditional, ceremonial figures, such as the Swordbearer, the City Marshal and the Serjeant-at-Arms.

The City of London viewed from the dome of St Paul's Cathedral.

23

Most of the ceremonial in the City centres round the **Lord Mayor**. The first one elected was Henry Fitz-Alwyn in 1192, and he held the position for twenty years. But he evidently outstayed his welcome, for it was decreed in 1215 that future Mayors would be elected annually, as they have been ever since. In that year King John granted the City of London the special privilege of electing its own Mayor, rather than having to accept a royal nominee. But he insisted that each new Lord Mayor must present himself to the King or his representatives at Westminster for royal approval, and this is still the procedure today.

The most famous Lord Mayor was probably Dick Whittington, who was first appointed in 1397 when his predecessor died in office. He was later elected three times – in 1397, 1406 and 1409. He may have had a cat, but he was hardly poor; he was a wealthy Mercer, who helped to finance the completion of Westminster Abbey, rebuilt Newgate Prison, paved Guildhall with Purbeck stone and did much for St Bartholomew's Hospital.

The Lord Mayor is the First Citizen within the City of London, with precedence immediately after the Sovereign; outside the City he ranks after Privy Councillors. The Lord Mayor is quite distinct from the Mayor of London, who has responsibilities affecting the whole of London rather than just the City and is elected for five years. The Lord Mayor is elected each year by the Court of Aldermen in Guildhall and is normally one of the two Sheriffs of the previous year. The nomination takes place on 29th September (Michaelmas Day), and he then presents himself in October to the Lord Chancellor at the House of Lords, where he receives royal approval of his appointment, as required by the Charter of 1215.

The new Lord Mayor takes office on the second Friday in November, when he and the outgoing Lord Mayor both take part in a public ceremony at Guildhall, known as the **Silent Change**, because it is traditionally conducted with hardly a word being spoken. The first step is that, as the Lord Mayor Elect gets up to be sworn in, the outgoing Lord Mayor quietly vacates his own chair and moves into that of his successor. This is followed by the transfer of the insignia, all done in silence. The outgoing Lord Mayor finally hands over his key to the City Seal Box, and from that moment the City of London has a new Lord Mayor, who is also Admiral of the Port of London. Trumpeters sound a fanfare, and church bells are rung as the two drive back to the Mansion House, with their positions reversed from the outward journey. Traditionally, there are no mayoral engagements that evening, so that everyone can rest before the Lord Mayor's Show the next day.

Officers of the City

Two important figures in all City ceremonial are the **Sheriffs**, who escort the Lord Mayor during his year of office. It is a most ancient appointment, which can be traced back to the seventh century, and candidates follow the same lengthy process of election as does the Lord Mayor, for one of the Sheriffs is traditionally selected as Lord Mayor.

The **Swordbearer** is 'the first esquire of the Lord Mayor's Household', with the duty of carrying the sword before his master on ceremonial occasions. His job is first mentioned in 1419, when it was laid down that he should be 'a man well bred (one who knows how in all places in that which unto such service pertains to support the honour of his lord and of the City)'. This still holds good, and today the Swordbearer is usually a retired Army officer.

The distinctive feature of his fifteenth-century uniform is the sable fur headdress known as the Cap of Maintenance. It has a concealed pocket, which holds the Lord Mayor's Key to the City Seal Box, and is worn on all ceremonial occasions, even in the presence of the Sovereign. It is, however, doffed on civic occasions when the Mace and Sword are laid on the table, and it is then placed beside them.

The **Common Cryer and Serjeant-at-Arms** (one person) is an office that was established well before 1338, when it was held by one

The Lord Mayor and his officials: (left to right) the Common Cryer and Serjeant-at-Arms; the Swordbearer; a Sheriff; the Lord Mayor; a Sheriff; the Mace Bearer and the City Marshal.

of the Royal Serjeants-at-Arms. He carries the Great Mace in front of the Lord Mayor and also justifies the first part of his title by making proclamations and announcements when required.

The third officer is the **City Marshal**, who often appears mounted, particularly on the Lord Mayor's Show, and also at Temple Bar, when it is his duty to challenge troops, Heralds and others who may not enter the City without leave from the Lord Mayor. His original role, under Letters Patent granted by Queen Elizabeth I, was to maintain law and order in the City, but his duties now are primarily ceremonial.

A key figure in all City ceremonial, but one who operates more behind the scenes, is the **City Remembrancer**, whose post also dates back to Elizabethan times. He is responsible for organising the many ceremonial events each year and guiding each new Lord Mayor through his elaborate routine. He also ensures that the ancient rights, privileges and traditions of the City are maintained as faithfully as possible in the face of changing times.

The Honourable Artillery Company

The military side of City ceremonial is largely in the hands of the Honourable Artillery Company, also known as the HAC. They are a volunteer unit of the Territorial and Army Volunteer Reserve, formerly the Territorial Army, and have always had close links with the City, their headquarters being at Armoury House in Moorfields.

They were formed by King Henry VIII in 1537, so they are the senior volunteer unit of the Army. Their original title was the Fraternity or Guild of St George, a body armed with longbows, crossbows and handguns. They later became known as the Artillery Company and acquired their present title in 1685.

Until 1778 only Freemen of the City were allowed to join and today the Company consists of businessmen from the City, who make it a highly efficient volunteer unit, with an operational role in the event of war. In peacetime they have a ceremonial role as well. In 1830 they were appointed by King William IV as his bodyguard in the City of London, and that royal duty has continued ever since, requiring them to provide escorts and guards of honour when the Sovereign visits the City.

They have also always traditionally escorted the Lord Mayor on ceremonial occasions within the City. For this role they formed in 1925 a 'Company of Pikemen and Musketeers', dressed in uniforms of 1641, with helmets and armour, and carrying the weapons of the time. They escort the Lord Mayor in his State Coach and are also in attendance at State Banquets and other functions. They may seem incongruous but they add much to the City's ceremonial, and membership is much sought after.

The Lord Mayor's coach, drawn by three pairs of Shire horses and with its escort of Pikemen and Musketeers.

Being an artillery regiment, they also have the duty of firing Royal Salutes at the Tower of London, even though this is not strictly within the bounds of the City (see chapter 10).

The livery companies

Another component in the ceremonial and tradition of the City is the livery companies. There are more than a hundred of them, some dating back ten centuries or more, while others have only recently been established. The Saddlers and the Butchers have documentary evidence of their existence in Saxon times. The Drapers and the Weavers both claim, less convincingly, that their skills show that they must have been around in the Garden of Eden, while the Founders go even further by taking as their motto 'God is the only Founder'.

The livery companies thrive on traditions and take pains to preserve ancient customs such as the passing of the loving cup at their ceremonial dinners. The Vintners and the Dyers take part in the ancient custom of Swan-upping on the Thames every July (see chapter 18). The Fishmongers organise Doggett's Coat and Badge Race, held on the Thames, and claimed to be the oldest, longest and toughest sculling race in the world (see chapter 18).

Daily events
5. The Queen's Life Guard

The Queen's Life Guard mounts daily at 11 a.m. at the Horse Guards building in Whitehall, and the ceremony lasts about half an hour. It normally takes place in the courtyard, but during the summer it is held on the parade ground, where there is more space for spectators.

The Queen's Life Guard is the oldest and most senior Royal Guard, dating back to 1660, when it was first mounted to protect King Charles II, who lived in Whitehall Palace, just over the road. It has remained the prerogative of the Household Cavalry ever since, and it may seem strange that they still mount guard in Whitehall, when the Sovereign is no longer there, but there is a good reason.

On 4th January 1689 one of King William III's Dutch laundresses left some clothes to dry too close to the fire, and by the next day Whitehall Palace was 'utterly burnt to the ground, nothing but walls and ruins left'. The Court moved to St James's Palace, but the Household Cavalry remained where they were in Whitehall, because the Horse Guards Arch was at that time the only access to the Palace

Guard Mounting at Horse Guards. In the foreground are The Blues and Royals in blue tunics and red plumes. Opposite them are The Life Guards with scarlet tunics and white plumes. The Trumpeters ride grey horses, a tradition dating back to the time of King James II, who ordered that they had to be readily identifiable in battle in order to receive the command to sound calls.

A Sovereign's Escort from The Life Guards with their Standard.

and Royal Park of St James and they continued to guard it. Today there are several approaches to Buckingham Palace, but the Arch is still the official State entrance, and therefore the Household Cavalry are still on duty.

On many State occasions the Royal Procession drives through Horse Guards Arch, but no one else is allowed to do so at any time, unless they are in possession of an Ivory Pass. The list of those granted this royal privilege is very limited, and all others, however important, will find their vehicle, even a bicycle, stopped by a stolid trooper with drawn sword, insisting on seeing an Ivory Pass.

The Queen's Life Guard is mounted by the two regiments of the Household Cavalry, usually on alternate days; so when the Guard changes you can see both The Life Guards in their scarlet tunics and white plumes and The Blues and Royals with their blue tunics and red plumes.

Two Farriers of the Household Cavalry with their ceremonial axes. The spike was used to despatch wounded horses in battle and the axe to cut off a hoof for identification.

When the Sovereign is in residence at Buckingham Palace, the Queen's Life Guard consists of one officer and fifteen other ranks, and a Standard is carried. This is called a 'Long Guard' and is changed to a 'Short Guard' of two non-commissioned officers and ten troopers with no Standard when The Queen is away from London, as indicated by the absence of the Royal Standard flying over Buckingham Palace.

The Guard sets out each day from its barracks on the south side of Hyde Park and rides from there to Horse Guards with a police escort. Near Hyde Park Corner on 20th July 1982 the Irish Republican Army exploded a car bomb as the Guard passed, killing three men and seven horses, but this has not stopped the ceremonial continuing.

All the Household Cavalry horses are traditionally black, except for those of the trumpeters, which are greys (see chapter 3).

When the New Guard arrives at Horse Guards, the two Guards form up facing each other, and after a formal exchange of compliments they wait while the sentries are changed. These consist of two mounted sentries in Whitehall, known as 'boxmen', and two dismounted sentries, one of whom guards the Arch, while the other is

One of the two mounted sentries in Whitehall, known as 'boxmen'.

on duty outside the guardroom. The two boxmen are on duty only between 10 a.m. and 4 p.m. and are relieved every hour, as the strain on both horse and rider is considerable, because of the constant feeding, fondling and photographing of the horse by sightseers.

Whenever the Sovereign drives through the Arch, as, for example, for a State Visit or the State Opening of Parliament, the Queen's Life Guard turns out and salutes. On one unfortunate occasion Queen Victoria appeared without warning, and the Guard failed to turn out, as it should have. The Queen thereupon angrily decreed that the Duty Officer at Hyde Park Barracks would ride down to Horse Guards and inspect the Guard every day for a hundred years. This was duly done and, although the hundred-year sentence has been completed, he still carries out his inspection at 4 p.m. whenever it is a Short Guard, with no officer, and thus also provides sightseers with a chance to see the Guard turn out.

6. Changing the Guard at Buckingham Palace

The Changing of the Guard at Buckingham Palace takes place in the forecourt at 11.30 a.m and lasts about forty-five minutes. The Guard normally mounts every day but may on occasions mount for forty-eight hours, if operational commitments are heavy. Also, in the event of rain or snow, it may carry out what is known as 'a wet weather mount' with no ceremonial.

When the Sovereign is in residence, the Guard consists of three officers and forty men, and the Queen's Colour is carried. At other times it is reduced to three officers and thirty-one men with the Regimental Colour. A laurel wreath is placed on the top of the colour pike on some days to mark either a royal anniversary or the anniversary of one of the battle honours of the regiment concerned.

The privilege of guarding the Sovereign's palace is the prerogative of the Foot Guards, who began the duty in 1689, when the Court moved from Whitehall to St James's Palace. The Guard Room is still in St James's Palace and the Guard is based there, although the well-known Changing of the Guard takes place in front of Buckingham Palace.

The band arrives at Buckingham Palace for the Changing of the Guard ceremony.

32

The Changing of the Guard. The band plays while the sentries are changed.

The pageantry of the ceremony is simple, but the setting, the tradition and the immaculate drill create an impressive scene. The Old Guard forms up in the forecourt and stands motionless, awaiting the arrival of its relief. The sound of military music grows louder, and then, precisely at 11.30, the New Guard swings in through the gate, led by a band. It halts facing the Old Guard, and they exchange compliments.

The two Captains now advance and carry out a symbolic handover of the keys of Buckingham Palace. There is then a pause while the sentries are changed at both palaces, and the band plays a selection of light music, the choice of which is the privilege of the Captain of the Old Guard. All concerned generally appreciate this interlude, but there is a story of one Director of Music in the 1920s who was playing music from a new operetta that was very popular at the time. He was delighted when a royal footman appeared carrying a message on a silver salver from King George V. He was less pleased, however, to read the note, which said: 'His Majesty does not know what the band has just played, but it is never to be played again.'

Once the sentries have changed over, the Old Guard marches off to Wellington Barracks, and the New Guard heads for St James's Palace to begin its tour of duty as the Queen's Guard.

Until 1959 the sentries at Buckingham Palace were positioned on the pavement outside the railings, but they were so pestered and harassed by sightseers that it was reluctantly decided to move the sentry boxes inside the forecourt; where they are today. At St James's Palace, however, they are not so protected and it is possible to obtain a close-up photograph there.

By day the sentries are purely ceremonial, but at night they become operational and patrol the grounds of Buckingham Palace, where they have on a number of occasions caught intruders and handed them over to the police, who are responsible for security.

Although three or four battalions of Foot Guards stationed in or near London take it in turn to find the duty each day, other units are increasingly being invited to take over temporarily, especially when the Guards are heavily committed on operations or training, in addition to their ceremonial commitments. On one occasion, when the Gurkhas took over, they found themselves standing next to guardsmen who in their bearskins towered a full 2 feet (60 cm) above them.

Bearskins were first worn in the eighteenth century in order to make the soldier look taller, and therefore more frightening to the enemy, and they were adapted for ceremonial use in 1832, when tunics similar to those worn today were also introduced.

It costs several thousand pounds nowadays to provide a full dress uniform, and so a 'pool' is maintained in London from which each Guards battalion, as it returns from duty overseas, can draw all its ceremonial clothing. This is particularly appreciated by the officers, who until the Second World War were required to pay for their own uniforms.

Ensigns marching with the colours at the Changing of the Guard at Buckingham Palace.

7. The Tower of London Guard

The Tower of London has been a Royal Palace and Fortress for more than nine centuries and was the residence of the Sovereign until Elizabethan times. It has its own ceremonial, and a Royal Guard mounts on Tower Green every day at noon. The Guard consists of one officer, five non-commissioned officers, a drummer and fifteen guardsmen and is usually provided by one of the five regiments of Foot Guards, although other units do take over on occasions.

It is not such an impressive scene as at Buckingham Palace, and there is no band, but it is an event worth seeing when visiting the Tower. The Guard normally mounts for twenty-four hours, and there are two sentries on duty, who also take part in the historic Ceremony of the Keys.

The Tower of London Guard, found by the Foot Guards.

The Ceremony of the Keys at the Tower of London. The Guard turns out and presents arms as the Chief Warder raises his bonnet and calls 'God preserve Queen Elizabeth', to which all respond 'Amen'.

8. The Ceremony of the Keys

The Ceremony of the Keys takes place at the Tower of London at 10 o'clock every evening.

From earliest times the gates of the Tower have been carefully locked at the end of the day, with no one being allowed in or out unless they knew the password. It is the duty of one of the Yeoman Warders to lock the gates and he has always been provided with a military escort to ensure that no one steals the Keys. This has developed into the unique Ceremony of the Keys.

Every night at exactly 9.53 the Chief Yeoman Warder appears from the Byward Tower, carrying in one hand a candle lantern and in the other the Queen's Keys. In front of the Bloody Tower he is joined by four members of the Tower Guard, one of whom takes over the lantern. The party then proceeds on its rounds, locking each of the gates leading from the Tower. The sentries present arms to the Keys as they pass, for they are regarded as representing the Sovereign.

As the escort returns to the Bloody Tower, they are challenged by the sentry there, and the following historic exchange takes place:

Sentry: 'Halt. Who comes there?'

Chief Warder: 'The Keys.'

Sentry: 'Whose Keys?'

Chief Warder: 'Queen Elizabeth's Keys.'

Sentry: 'Pass, Queen Elizabeth's Keys. All's well.'

The Escort to the Keys then proceeds through the Bloody Tower archway to the steps beyond, where the complete Tower Guard has turned out. As the party halts, the Guard presents arms. The Chief Warder takes two paces forward, raises his bonnet and calls out 'God preserve Queen Elizabeth', to which the Guard and the Yeoman Warders all respond 'Amen'.

As the clock strikes the first note of ten o'clock the drummer sounds Last Post and the Chief Warder marches off to lodge the Keys in the Queen's House for the night. From midnight no one can enter the Tower unless they know the password.

The Ceremony of the Keys has taken place in peace and war without interruption for over seven hundred years. It was even continued throughout the Blitz of 1940–1, and on 16th April 1941 a bomb landed within the Tower so close to the Escort that they were blown off their feet. But they picked themselves up, reformed and completed their rounds, thus maintaining the unbroken record.

Admission to the Ceremony of the Keys is by ticket only as there is very limited space for spectators. Applications for tickets should be made through travel agents or direct to the authorities at the Tower of London.

Annual events

9. State Visits

State Visits by rulers of friendly countries have throughout the ages provided an excuse for scenes of splendid pageantry as monarchs have sought not only to offer a worthy welcome to their guests, but also at the same time to create a favourable impression of their own power and prestige. One of the outstanding historical examples was the Field of the Cloth of Gold, when Henry VIII of England and Francis I of France met near Calais in June 1520. It was a meeting of two of the most powerful and magnificent princes in Europe, and each was determined to outshine the other.

Henry and his court sailed from Dover in the *Henry Grace à Dieu*, with sails painted gold, escorted by an impressive fleet and accompanied by 2865 horses and 3997 followers, including almost the entire nobility of his realm. On arrival at the Val d'Or, they found a complete tented city set up for them; there were tents designed as palaces, and one, painted to look like brick, contained a huge gilded banqueting hall. The celebrations continued for nineteen days, with

The Guard of Honour on a State Visit is inspected by the King of Norway.

The Queen with her guest on a State Visit riding in an open carriage with a Household Cavalry Escort.

tournaments, displays, feasting and other entertainments.

The ceremonial today is on a more modest scale. A State Visit in its present form is a comparatively modern practice, dating back only to the beginning of the nineteenth century, and there were no official visits by monarchs of other countries during the two previous centuries.

The first State Visit on modern lines was a gathering of the sovereigns of the Grand Alliance in 1814 after the exile of Napoleon Bonaparte to Elba. It lasted just under three weeks and alternated between London and Windsor, where the royal guests were installed as Knights of the Garter and spent an afternoon at Ascot Races. There were banquets, and their stay culminated in a military review in Hyde Park and a naval review at Spithead. There were then no more State Visits until that of King Frederick William III of Prussia in 1842, but after that they took place on average every five years until the end of the nineteenth century.

There are now normally two a year, one in the spring and one in the summer or autumn, and they last three to five days. Guests are invited either to London or Windsor, and on rare occasions to Edinburgh.

In London a State Visit usually starts with a Reception on Horse

Guards Parade. A Guard of Honour, one hundred strong, is mounted by the Foot Guards, and it is customary for the Captain to report 'Guard ready for your inspection' in the language of the guest. It is a nice gesture, provided that the visitor does not prolong the conversation, in which case the help of an interpreter may be required.

The Reception over, a Carriage Procession is formed for the State Drive along the Royal Route to Buckingham Palace or Windsor Castle, which is a chance for the public to see something of the splendour.

There is a set pattern for a Royal Procession, whether on a State Visit or some other occasion. It is led by the Outriders, who may be either police, royal grooms or troopers of the Household Cavalry. Then comes the First Division of the Sovereign's Escort, officers and men of the Household Cavalry riding ahead of and round The Queen's carriage. There will usually be several other carriages in the Procession, and behind them the Second Division of the Escort.

At Buckingham Palace The Queen's Guard turns out, and the Procession drives into the forecourt. There is little more to be seen by those watching, but this is far from being the end of the ceremonial. As The Queen's guest enters the palace, the steps are lined by dismounted troopers of the Household Cavalry, and the Lord Chamberlain and the Lord Steward await the royal party, carrying their wands of office. The Gentlemen at Arms form yet another Guard of Honour, resplendent in their plumed helmets and with their Standard. Beyond them are the Yeomen of the Guard with their Colour.

That evening there will be a State Banquet (see chapter 19) and during the next three or four days there will be further ceremonial occasions, and the visiting Head of State customarily gives a return banquet with The Queen as his guest. There will also be visits to Number 10 Downing Street, and probably to factories and businesses, for State Visits today, impressive and historic though they may be, are also of considerable political and economic significance.

10. Royal Salutes

It has long been customary to salute distinguished guests and also to celebrate anniversaries by the firing of gun salutes. In London Royal Salutes are fired on specified days every year in honour of certain royal anniversaries, which are:

The Queen's actual Birthday (21st April)

The Queen's Official Birthday (second Saturday in June)

The Birthday of the Duke of Edinburgh (10th June)

The Anniversary of Accession Day (6th February)

The Anniversary of Coronation Day (2nd June).

Salutes are also fired on unspecified dates for the State Opening of Parliament, the Proroguing of Parliament and State Visits.

In London salutes are fired at two spots, Hyde Park and the Tower of London, which are both excellent for watching this impressive ceremony. In Hyde Park it is the duty of the King's Troop of the Royal Horse Artillery, a Regular Army unit based in London at St John's Wood. Dressed in uniforms of the early nineteenth century, they gallop their seventy-one horses into action as if on the field of battle in Napoleonic days, and the six 13-pounders are manhandled into position. It is a dramatic sight, taking place as it does in the heart of London.

The unit retains the proud title of 'The King's Troop' even when the Sovereign is a Queen. Their original title was 'The Riding Troop', and when King George VI visited them on 24th October 1947 he was asked to sign the Visitors' Book in the Officers' Mess. As he did so, he paused, struck out the word 'Riding' and inserted in its place 'King's'. And so it has remained, for Queen Elizabeth II on her Accession expressed the wish that it should continue unchanged during her reign in memory of her father and his affection for the Royal Horse Artillery.

Salutes at the Tower of London are fired by the Honourable Artillery Company, which is a volunteer unit (see chapter 4). They do not have horses but are nevertheless a fine sight as they come into action against the background of Tower Bridge.

The number of rounds fired varies according to the occasion and also the place where the salute takes place. There are many variations and subtleties, but the basic Royal Salute is twenty-one rounds and an extra twenty rounds are added by the King's Troop because Hyde Park is a Royal Park, thus making a total of forty-one. At the Tower of London sixty-two rounds are normally fired rather than forty-one; twenty-one for the Royal Salute, twenty more because the Tower is a

The firing of Royal Salutes in Hyde Park is the responsibility of The King's Troop, Royal Horse Artillery, dressed in uniforms of the early nineteenth century. (Above) Some of their seventy-one horses gallop into position. (Below) The Salute is fired with six 13-pounder guns.

A Royal Salute being fired at the Tower of London by the Honourable Artillery Company.

Royal Palace and Fortress, and then an additional twenty-one 'for the City of London', a practice begun about 1828 as the City's tribute to the Sovereign.

The Tower probably holds the record for the largest number of rounds fired at one time, with a total of 124 rounds in those years when the Queen's Official Birthday coincides with Prince Philip's birthday on 10th June.

Rounds are fired at intervals of ten seconds, by each gun in turn, and there is a special drill for a misfire, which ensures that the timing of the Salute is barely upset.

The first round of a Royal Salute (other than for State Visits) is normally fired at noon, but at the Tower of London it is at 1 p.m. This is because the officers and men of The Honourable Artillery Company are part-time soldiers, who mostly work in the City, and it is more convenient for them to leave their desks at lunchtime.

Celebratory flags on Horse Guards Road.

11. Guard Mounting from Horse Guards

A little known but nonetheless very impressive ceremonial occasion in London is Guard Mounting from Horse Guards, which takes place at around 10 a.m. on about eight mornings in late May every year. It is a revival of the practice of the eighteenth and nineteenth centuries when both the Household Cavalry and the Foot Guards used to form up their Royal Guards on Horse Guards, because it was the most convenient open space, and then marched from there to their respective guardrooms. This continued until Wellington Barracks were built in 1834, after which the Foot Guards paraded there for Guard Mounting.

It is in effect a miniature version of Trooping the Colour and is a fine sight, although the Household Cavalry do not take part.

On this parade the officers are made to take up their positions by marching across the parade ground with drawn swords in slow time – the traditional test of sobriety and fitness for duty after any social activities the night before. This is a revival of a custom that dates from George II's reign (1727–60).

The stands erected for the Trooping are probably in position but only one is available for watching Guard Mounting, and the best place to go is probably in St James's Park near the Guards Memorial.

44

The Massed Bands of the Foot Guards in front of the Guards Memorial at Beating Retreat.

12. Beating Retreat

During the first two weeks of June, the ceremony of Beating Retreat takes place on Horse Guards Parade on three or four evenings each week. The 7500 seats erected for the Queen's Birthday Parade are available, and the proceeds go to Service charities.

The Mounted Bands of the Household Cavalry and the Massed Bands of the Foot Guards, four hundred strong, are a stirring sight marching and playing against the background of St James's Park. Some of the performances are in the early evening and some are late, so that they can be floodlit. The Royal Marines and other regiments also use Horse Guards to Beat Retreat during this period, so there is a wide choice.

The custom of Beating Retreat has its origins in the sixteenth century, when the drummers of garrisons sounded it at the end of the day. It gave warning either that the gates were about to be shut or that it was time for the guard to mount. This developed in the eighteenth century into the more formal ceremonial we know today, denoting the end of the working day and time for guard mounting.

13. Trooping the Colour

The most impressive military parade in the world is undoubtedly the 'Ceremony of Trooping the Colour held on the occasion of The Queen's Birthday'. It takes place on the second Saturday in June to celebrate the official Birthday of the Sovereign and is carried out by her personal troops, the Household Division, on Horse Guards Parade, with The Queen herself attending and taking the salute.

The custom of Trooping the Colour (it is incorrect to call it 'The Trooping of the Colour') dates back to the time of Charles II in the seventeenth century when the Colours of a regiment were used as a rallying point in battle and were therefore trooped in front of the soldiers every day to make sure that every man could recognise those of his own regiment. In London the Foot Guards used to do this from 1755 onwards as part of their daily Guard Mounting on Horse Guards (see chapter 11) and the ceremonial of the present parade is along similar lines.

In 1805 the parade was for the first time carried out to celebrate the Sovereign's birthday, and the custom has continued ever since. It was originally held on the actual day, which was satisfactory until the end of Queen Victoria's long reign, as her birthday fell conveniently on

The Household Cavalry walk past The Queen on the Trooping the Colour Parade. In the foreground are the Massed Bands of the Foot Guards and the Mounted Bands of the Household Cavalry.

24th May. But her successor, Edward VII, was born in November, and he therefore decreed that he would also have an official birthday, which would be celebrated on 10th June. This continued until 1959, when, to avoid the increasing traffic problems caused by holding such a parade on a weekday, it was changed to 'a Saturday early in June'.

Queen Victoria never attended the parade herself, but throughout the twentieth century the Sovereign has nearly always taken the salute in person, either mounted or from an open carriage. Since 1987 The Queen has attended in a carriage rather than riding, which she did before that on thirty-six occasions, riding side-saddle and wearing the uniform of the regiment whose Colour was being trooped.

Over one thousand officers and men are on parade, together with two hundred horses; 450 musicians from ten bands and corps of drums march and play as one. Some 113 words of command are given by the Officer in command of the Parade, and there is no scope for error with the television cameras recording every move.

Since 1998 the King's Troop, Royal Horse Artillery, have taken part in the parade, and when they ride past the Sovereign, they exercise their right to precede even the Household Cavalry, which they are entitled to do when they have their guns with them.

Only two rehearsals are held, which is the absolute minimum for such a complex parade, particularly as some of the battalions taking part may have returned from active operations abroad only two or three months before. Within that time bearskins must be issued and tunics fitted; ceremonial drill must replace battle drills, and the special intricacies of the Trooping must be learned, in addition to routine duties. It is a challenging task, but it is achieved.

On the morning of the Trooping, from 10.20 onwards the Guards, each consisting of three officers and seventy men, march on to Horse Guards Parade and form up. Number 1 Guard, which is the Escort for the Colour, is the last to arrive and takes the place of honour on the right flank.

Originally all the men on parade used to receive an extra day's pay to celebrate the royal birthday, but today only those mounting The Queen's Guard are rewarded – by the sum of just 50 pence. It is well earned.

Precisely as the clock on the Horse Guards Building strikes eleven, the Royal Procession arrives and The Queen takes the Royal Salute. It is a magnificent sight in a unique setting, with St James's Park and the dramatic white outline of the Guards Memorial as the background. Until the Second World War the military attachés of foreign and Commonwealth countries used to attend on horseback and their varied uniforms added considerably to the colour.

A view of the final moments of The Queen's Birthday Parade. The Household Cavalry have just walked past The Queen and are passing behind the rigid lines of the Foot Guards before trotting past. In the background are the Guards Memorial and St James's Park.

The parade begins with the Inspection, The Queen driving slowly down the ranks of all the Guards, and then past the Household Cavalry. As she resumes her position, the Officer Commanding gives the single dramatic word of command, 'Troop'. After a brief pause, the Massed Bands strike up the traditional air 'Les Huguenots', to which they slow-march across the parade ground and march back in quick time.

Now comes what is perhaps the most solemn and symbolic moment of the parade, as the Escort alone marches forward, ready to take over the Colour. Whatever the regiment finding the Escort, the march played at this moment is 'The British Grenadiers', because the right flank company of every battalion was traditionally the 'grenadier company', consisting of the biggest and strongest men.

The Regimental Sergeant Major, who never draws his sword except on this occasion, now takes over the Colour from the Sergeant and in turn hands it over to the Ensign, the junior officer who will carry it for the rest of the parade.

The Colour, now guarded by the whole Escort, is then trooped in slow time down the ranks of all the Guards, for every man to see, at the end of which the Escort resumes its original position, but with the Colour now in its custody.

The actual Trooping is over, but the parade is not, for the Guards have still to march past their Sovereign. This is a welcome moment, for they have now been on parade for some two hours and have been standing rigidly to attention for the last thirteen minutes or so – an effort that few of those watching would want to undertake.

First, the Foot Guards march past in slow and quick time. Then it is the turn at last of The King's Troop and the Household Cavalry, who have waited in the background for an hour. Until 1950 the Household Cavalry used to walk past first, but the Foot Guards, not unreasonably, objected to having to march through the droppings inevitably left by

After Trooping the Colour the Massed Bands return down The Mall to Buckingham Palace.

the horses, and the present procedure was agreed.

First, the King's Troop walk and trot past with their guns, and then come the four Divisions of the Sovereign's Escort of the Household Cavalry.

There is an elegant panache about the gleaming horses, glittering cuirasses, flowing plumes and jangling bridles. There then follows an even more stirring sight as they break into a trot and rank past again to the jingling rhythm of the 'Keel Row'. It is very fine horsemanship and also a fitting climax to The Queen's Birthday Parade, which ends with a final Royal Salute.

But the ceremonial is not yet over, for The Queen now leads her Household Troops back down The Mall to Buckingham Palace, where they march past once again.

So ends the ceremonial of The Queen's Birthday Parade, surely one of the finest spectacles in the world, but it is not the end for those who are watching outside Buckingham Palace. First, the usual ceremony of Changing the Guard takes place, the New Guard being the Escort, which has just trooped its Colour on Horse Guards.

Then at 1 p.m. The Queen and the Royal Family make one of their popular appearances on the balcony of Buckingham Palace, this time to watch the Royal Air Force pay its birthday tribute with a fly-past down The Mall.

It is difficult to obtain tickets for the Birthday Parade, though some are available by ballot, but they are available for the first and second rehearsals, which take place on the two preceding Saturdays. Write to Headquarters Household Division, Horse Guards, Whitehall, London SW1, before 1st March.

It is possible to see the parade from St James's Park or to watch the processions in The Mall. The best position other than Horse Guards is probably outside Buckingham Palace, where one can see the ceremonial that takes place there before and after the parade.

14. The State Opening of Parliament

Each year the Sovereign drives in State to Westminster for the State Opening of Parliament. This is usually in November, but it may take place at other times, or even more than once a year if there is a change of government.

The ceremony takes place in the House of Lords, and the Commons are summoned to hear 'The Queen's Speech from the Throne', formally opening the next session of her Parliament and setting out the policies of her Government. There is room for only a very few spectators inside the Palace of Westminster, and tickets are difficult to obtain, but through television the ceremony has been made available to everyone.

The Queen travels from Buckingham Palace to Westminster along the Royal Route, using the Irish State Coach, drawn by four horses. She has her usual 'Escort of the Household Cavalry', and the whole route is guarded by street liners, who present arms as the Royal Procession passes. Military bands play light music, so there is plenty to see and hear.

Several events occur before the actual State Opening, and The Queen is the last person to drive down the Royal Route. First comes a Guard of Honour of the Foot Guards, one hundred strong, on its way to the House of Lords, where it forms up.

Then comes a solitary carriage, usually Queen Alexandra's State Coach, with a special mounted escort of a corporal of horse and six troopers from the Household Cavalry. This contains the Regalia, which, having been collected from the Jewel House at the Tower of London, are taken to Buckingham Palace and then escorted to Westminster for use at the State Opening.

The Imperial State Crown is carried by the Comptroller of the Lord Chamberlain's Office, while the Assistant Comptroller bears the Cap of Maintenance. The Sword of State is carried by a specially appointed Gentleman Usher, and the street liners pay compliments to the Regalia as they pass by, showing the symbolic respect due to them.

Various members of the Royal Family arrive by car, and before the Royal Procession sets out, the cellars of the Houses of Parliament are searched by the Yeomen of the Guard. This custom dates back to 5th November 1605, when the notorious villain Guy Fawkes tried as part of a Papist plot to blow up the Houses of Parliament. He was caught in the nick of time by the Yeomen of the Guard, and ever since a detachment of ten Yeomen has ceremoniously searched the cellars in

The Irish State Coach carries The Queen and the Duke of Edinburgh to the State Opening of Parliament.

The Royal Standard flies from Victoria Tower while The Queen is within the Palace of Westminster.

case such a plot is hatched again. Today, because of the risk of terrorism, the lanterns of the Yeomen have to be reinforced by sniffer dogs, metal detectors and similar devices, but the tradition is maintained.

As The Queen arrives at the Sovereign's Entrance to the House of Lords, the Royal Standard is unfurled on the Victoria Tower, replacing the Union Flag, and it remains there while Her Majesty is within the palace. The Sovereign is received by the Earl Marshal and also by the Lord Great Chamberlain, who, as Keeper of the Royal Palace of Westminster, wears scarlet Court Dress and has hanging at his hip the golden key to the palace. As The Queen moves up the Royal Staircase to the Robing Chamber, she passes between two lines of dismounted troopers of the Household Cavalry in full dress with drawn swords – one of the occasions when they provide what is known as a Staircase Party and exercise their privilege of being the only troops allowed to bear arms within the Royal Palaces.

The Royal Procession, as it makes its way slowly through the Royal Gallery to the Chamber of the House of Lords, contains a unique selection of historic titles from national pageantry. It is led by the Heralds and Pursuivants, followed by members of the Royal Household such as the Crown Equerry and the Keeper of Her Majesty's Privy Purse. Then come the Earl Marshal and the Lord

The carriage with the Royal Mace leaves the Houses of Parliament after the State Opening.

Great Chamberlain, both walking backwards ahead of the Sovereign. Behind the Royal Family come more officers of the Royal Household and of the Royal Bodyguards.

In the House of Lords, the peers and peeresses are all in their robes, with the peeresses wearing tiaras. The Lords Spiritual are there in their ecclesiastical robes, and the bewigged Judges are sitting in the centre on their traditional Woolsack.

The Sovereign sits on the throne, with the Duke of Edinburgh on her left and the Prince of Wales on her right. Other members of the Royal Family sit on the front benches nearest the throne.

The Lord Chancellor now advances and, removing the Queen's Speech from a special silk bag, hands it to the Sovereign but, before it is read, the 'faithful Commons' must be summoned to attend and hear the contents.

This is the moment when a traditional ritual is carried out to remind all concerned of the rights of the House of Commons and of the abuse of these rights by King Charles I. It dates back to November 1641, when Charles, having ruled without any Parliament for eleven years, refused to accept John Pym's Grand Remonstrance demanding more rights for Parliament. When Pym stood firm, the King entered the

House of Commons on 4th January 1642 with troops, intending to arrest the five Members most closely involved in what he regarded as treason. They had, however, escaped, and he was forced to withdraw empty-handed.

The Gentleman Usher of the Black Rod, in his capacity as the Sovereign's Messenger, makes his way to the House of Commons. As he approaches, the Serjeant-at-Arms there deliberately slams the door in his face. Black Rod then knocks three times and, when the door is eventually opened, he conveys his message: 'Mr Speaker, The Queen commands this Honourable House to attend Her Majesty immediately in the House of Peers.'

With a traditional lack of haste, the Commons, led by the Speaker and the Serjeant-at-Arms bearing his Mace, proceed to the House of Lords, deliberately loitering and chatting casually as they approach, just to show that they stand in no awe of the 'other place'.

Not all the Members of Parliament attend, for there would not be room, so a representative group stands at the far end of the Chamber opposite the throne and listens as The Queen reads 'The Most Gracious Speech from the Throne'. It ends with the words 'I pray that the blessing of Almighty God may rest upon your counsels', and Parliament is now formally opened.

The Royal Procession re-forms and leaves the Chamber, returning shortly afterwards in a carriage procession to Buckingham Palace. The Guard of Honour returns to barracks, the street liners disperse, and the ceremonial of the State Opening of Parliament is completed.

It is possible to watch the various processions from anywhere along the Royal Route, but the best place is probably outside the House of Lords, where you can also see the Guard of Honour, the Royal Procession and all the other comings and goings.

15. The Lord Mayor's Show

The most spectacular ceremonial event in the City is the Lord Mayor's Show. It takes place on the second Saturday in November and is the occasion when the new Lord Mayor, elected only the day before, 'shows' himself to the citizens – hence the title.

The historic reason for the procession is that the Lord Mayor must go to the Royal Courts of Justice in the Strand to be sworn in before the Lord Chief Justice and the Judges of the Queen's Bench Division. This custom dates back to 1215, when King John gave the citizens of the City of London the special privilege of electing their own Lord Mayor rather than having to accept a royal nominee. The King did, however, insist that each Lord Mayor should present himself to the Monarch at Westminster for royal approval. If the King was away, which he often was, the Lord Mayor was to report to the Justices, which is what happens today.

From the mid fifteenth century the journey to Westminster was usually made by river, and it gradually developed into quite a procession, as some of the livery companies accompanied the Lord Mayor on their own barges and improvised displays to enliven the trip.

On the return journey, the Lord Mayor had to ride on horseback from Blackfriars Bridge, where he disembarked, to Guildhall, and in 1710 Sir Gilbert Heathcote was unseated from his horse. It was then decided that it would be safer and more dignified for the Lord Mayor to travel this last stage by coach, and this became the custom.

The Lord Mayor's Show is a spectacular colourful procession, but it is not just a jollification. It consists primarily of a number of floats, based on a central theme selected by the Lord Mayor, with the serious purpose of publicising the business achievements of the City. Floats and displays are prepared by the livery companies and other organisations; there are bands and detachments from all three Services, and the Household Cavalry provides a mounted detachment with their Mounted Band, both in State Dress.

Some fifty floats, twenty-three bands and 3500 people take part in the Show; there is no rehearsal, and so it is quite an achievement of organisation. The highlight is undoubtedly the Lord Mayor himself in his magnificent gold State Coach, with his traditional escort of pikemen and musketeers from the Honourable Artillery Company, and the City Marshal riding ahead of him.

The impressive State Coach was built in 1757 for the then Lord Mayor, Sir Charles Asgil, at a cost of £1065 0s 3d. It weighs over 3

The Lord Mayor's Coach with his guard of pikemen in the Lord Mayor's Show.

tons and is drawn by three pairs of Shire horses. It is normally used only for the Lord Mayor's Show and at Coronations, and is on display at other times in the Museum of London. The full length of the coach is 65 feet (19.8 metres), and it calls for considerable skill to manoeuvre and control it. It is also an uncomfortable ride, as the suspension consists of just four leather braces fastened to the body by four thick leather buckles.

The coach carrying the previous Lord Mayor – known as the Late Lord Mayor – is escorted by Yeoman Warders.

The procession starts at Guildhall and passes the Mansion House, where the Lord Mayor watches from a balcony and takes the salute. He then joins in for the ride down Fleet Street. After the swearing-in ceremony, the return journey is along the Embankment.

The Times commented rather sourly in 1867 that the Lord Mayor's Show was 'a street nuisance and nothing more', which made the City 'a standing object of ridicule to men of the world'. Happily, this is certainly not the case today, and it is not only one of London's leading ceremonial events, but also evidence of the business achievements of the City of London.

The Queen at the Remembrance Service at the Cenotaph.

16. Remembrance Sunday

No ceremony is celebrated throughout Britain so sincerely and so universally as Remembrance Sunday, the second Sunday in November. This is the day when the whole nation pays homage to the million and a half men and women who died in two World Wars.

The focal point of the nation's tribute is the Cenotaph in Whitehall, designed by Sir Edwin Lutyens and inscribed with only three words, 'The Glorious Dead'.

On Remembrance Sunday it is the scene of solemn and deeply moving ceremonial. Formed up round it are detachments from all the Armed Forces and also the civilian services. The Massed Bands of the Royal Marines, the Foot Guards and the Royal Air Force play solemn music in keeping with the spirit of the occasion.

To the north of the Cenotaph stand the ranks of ex-servicemen, medals proudly pinned across their chests. The pavements are lined by silent crowds, while from windows in the Home Office members of the Royal Family watch the scene below.

The First World War ended at the eleventh hour of the eleventh day of the eleventh month of 1918 and every year thereafter at that hour on that date a Two Minute Silence was held throughout the United Kingdom to commemorate that moment; but from 1956 this Day of Remembrance was changed from 11th November to the second

The Cenotaph with wreaths laid on Remembrance Sunday.

Sunday in November, that being considered more appropriate.

A few moments before eleven, The Queen appears and takes up her position facing the Cenotaph. As Big Ben, only a few hundred yards away, sounds the first stroke of eleven o'clock, a gun of The King's Troop, Royal Horse Artillery, on Horse Guards Parade fires a single round.

It is the start of the Two Minute Silence, and suddenly the heart of

London comes to a halt. It is not only an act of remembrance but also one of dedication, when those who are still alive undertake to try to be worthy of those who died. It is also a moment of unusual national unity, when men, women and children of all ages, colours, classes and creeds join in a common aim of seeking peace in a troubled world.

The boom of the second round of gunfire breaks the silence, and bugles sound the Last Post. The Queen steps forward and lays a wreath of red poppies at the foot of the Cenotaph, the first of many from the Royal Family, the governments of the United Kingdom and the Commonwealth countries, from the Services and other organisations.

The Bishop of London leads a simple service, which includes the hymn for ever associated with this occasion, 'O God, Our Help in Ages Past'. The choir, which is the Gentlemen and Children of The Chapel Royal in their scarlet and gold, adds a touch of colour to the otherwise sombre scene of grey, black and blue.

After the service, Reveille is sounded, the National Anthem is played, and The Queen and those who laid wreaths depart.

The finale is perhaps the most moving moment of all, as the thousand or so ex-servicemen march past the Cenotaph, to the tunes they knew so long ago: 'Tipperary', 'There's a Long, Long Trail A-winding' and 'Take Me Back to Dear Old Blighty'. Their pace is slow, one hundred to the minute, but their step is steady and their shoulders are squared, as they turn to salute the memorial to their comrades in arms, those who 'gave their tomorrow for our today'.

Ex-servicemen march past the Cenotaph after the Remembrance Day ceremony.

17. Royal Visits to the City

Ever since it received its first Royal Charter in 1067 from William the Conqueror, the City of London has jealously maintained its 'rights and privileges'. It does not, for example, allow any troops to march through its streets without special permission from the Lord Mayor.

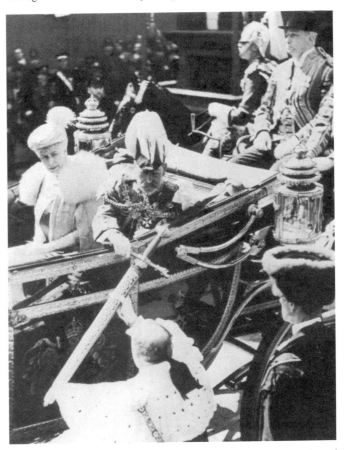

King George V touches the hilt of the City Sword as he enters the City of London at Temple Bar. The Sword is being presented by the Lord Mayor, behind whom stands the Swordbearer, wearing his sable Cap of Maintenance.

There is also a long-established custom whereby even the Sovereign, when visiting the City, halts at the City boundary and is met there by the Lord Mayor and a deputation of City dignitaries. This is not, as is often thought, intended to show that the City has the power to prevent the Sovereign from entering without the Lord Mayor's approval. Rather, it is the reverse, for it is an occasion when the City demonstrates its allegiance and loyalty to the Crown.

The ceremony usually takes place at Temple Bar in Fleet Street, which marks the City limit on the road to Westminster. When the Sovereign is due to make a State entry into the City, a red cord is stretched across the road to symbolise the gateway of Temple Bar. The gateway itself was taken down and moved out of London in 1878 because it caused traffic problems.

Behind the Lord Mayor stands the Swordbearer, with the Pearl Sword, said to have been presented to the City by Queen Elizabeth I. A City Sword is normally carried in front of the Lord Mayor, but in the event of a Royal Visit, it is customarily handed over to the Sovereign for the duration of the visit, as a sign of the royal overlordship. But in 1641, when King Charles I entered the City of London, he just touched the sword when it was presented to him and then gave it back to the Lord Mayor. So a new tradition was established and has continued ever since.

So today, as the Royal Procession approaches Temple Bar, the cord is withdrawn, and the royal carriage or car halts just within the City boundary. The Lord Mayor takes over the sword from the Swordbearer, and presents the hilt to the Sovereign, who touches it and then signifies that it is to be retained by the Lord Mayor. It is then the duty of the Lord Mayor to carry the sword in front of his Sovereign, and he will be seen doing so as he precedes The Queen up the steps of St Paul's for some State occasion there.

18. Thames Traditions

The river Thames was until the middle of the nineteenth century a main thoroughfare of London and a scene of constant activity. Royalty and the nobility had their own craft for travelling up and down the river, as did the Lord Mayor and the livery companies of the City of London. London Bridge was until 1760 the only crossing place for land transport.

Great ceremonial occasions were often staged on the Thames, which provided a finer setting than most places in the capital. In 1487, for example, there was a display of great splendour when Henry VII's Queen Elizabeth came from Greenwich by barge for her coronation at Westminster; Anne Boleyn did the same for her coronation in 1533. The Stuarts particularly enjoyed lavish river pageants, and a spectacular *Aqua Triumphalis* was staged in 1662 when Catharine of Braganza arrived from Portugal to marry King Charles II.

Today there is little ceremonial on the Thames, though in 1977 there was a River Progress to celebrate the Silver Jubilee and a firework display was held, accompanied by Handel's *Water Music*. There was another in 2002 for The Queen's Golden Jubilee.

Some traditions, however, are kept alive; there are still Bargemasters and Watermen of the Thames, and two annual events are held on the river, Swan-upping, and Doggett's Coat and Badge Race.

Bargemasters and Watermen

Although the State barges are now all in museums, five Bargemasters still exist, the most senior being the Queen's Bargemaster. The others are retained by four livery companies, the Fishmongers, the Vintners, the Dyers, and the Guild of Watermen and Lightermen.

The Sovereign also still maintains twenty-four Royal Watermen as a continuation of one of the most ancient appointments in the Royal Household. The earliest Royal Palace was at Westminster, with others at the Tower of London, Greenwich, Sheen, Hampton Court and Windsor; all were close to the river and more easily accessible by boat than by road, so the Royal Watermen were fully employed.

Their uniform, in royal scarlet, is still the skirted-tunic style of the traditional Thames Waterman, with a dark blue cap, scarlet stockings, a white shirt and black shoes. On the front and back they bear large solid silver badges with the Royal Cypher. The uniform of the Queen's Bargemaster is distinctive in that he wears a tailcoat jacket with additional braid, and his stockings are white rather than scarlet.

Two Watermen in the Lord Mayor's Procession.

The duties of the Royal Watermen are now purely ceremonial, and they took part, for example, in the 1977 and 2002 River Progresses. They also have some duties ashore, acting as boxmen on royal carriages on State occasions.

A regular and significant duty for them is at the State Opening of Parliament, when the Queen's Bargemaster and four Royal Watermen travel as boxmen on Queen Alexandra's Coach to guard the Crown when it is transported from Buckingham Palace to Westminster and back. This is a reminder of the time when they were responsible for bringing it direct to Westminster by boat from the Tower of London.

The appointment of Royal Waterman does not bring great wealth, the pay being £3.50 a year, but it is a much sought-after honour that carries on a long-established tradition on the Thames.

Swan-upping

Through the ages, the swan has been regarded as a royal bird, and all those on the open Thames, and indeed elsewhere, have by common law belonged to the Sovereign. The penalty for killing a royal bird has always been severe, and as late as the mid nineteenth century it was deportation for seven years. In the fifteenth century, however, the Sovereign allowed two livery companies, the Vintners and the Dyers, to own a number of swans each. As a result it has been necessary ever since to mark the cygnets on the Thames every year in order to identify them, and this has become the ceremony of Swan-upping.

On the Monday of the third week in July a group of six Thames skiffs sets off from Temple Stairs at Blackfriars on a six-day Swan Voyage up the Thames as far as Henley in Oxfordshire. They are led by the Queen's Swan Keeper, who is accompanied by the Swan Master of the Dyers' Company and the Swan Marker of the Vintners' Company; both are officers of their companies nominated for the post.

All concerned wear traditional uniforms, and each boat flies the

Boats forming a 'V' shape to trap the swans during the annual Swan-upping on the river Thames.

banner of its owners. The rowing is done by the Swan-uppers, so called because the first man to see a brood of swans traditionally shouts 'All-up', to warn the other boats to manoeuvre in order to surround them. When they are all caught, the cygnets are marked, and the whole brood is then released; they used to be pinioned, but this practice was abandoned in 1978.

The Queen's swans are not marked at all; those of the Dyers have one small nick made on the right side of the beak, and the Vintners' swans have two nicks made, one on each side of the beak. It is a skilled job and is carried out today in consultation with the Royal Society for the Prevention of Cruelty to Animals, to prevent any harm to the birds.

The Swan-uppers work their way steadily upstream to Henley, the customary end of the Swan Voyage. As they pass Windsor Castle, they stand to attention in their boats and, with oars raised, salute 'Her Majesty The Queen, Seigneur of the Swans'.

The duties of the Queen's Swan Keeper and his three Swan Herdsmen do not end at Swan-upping. They turn out at all hours to tend injured or strayed swans, they feed birds during the winter, and look after them throughout the year.

In the sixteenth and seventeenth centuries Swan-upping was purely a routine job, but it then became a social occasion for the livery companies, with barges bringing guests to watch the proceedings, to be entertained by hired musicians, and to enjoy much eating and drinking. Swan-upping has always been one of the many and varied responsibilities of the Lord Chamberlain, who regards it as a valuable function to record and safeguard the swan population on the Thames. The Courts of the Dyers' and Vintners' companies also take a close interest and still follow the Swan-uppers by launch on one day of the Swan Voyage. Later in the year both companies also hold Swan Feasts at which roast swan traditionally appears on the menu and is eaten with due ceremony.

Doggett's Coat and Badge Race

Another continuing tradition on the Thames is Doggett's Coat and Badge Race, rowed every year over a 4½ mile (7.25 km) stretch of the river from the Old Swan at London Bridge to the White Swan at Chelsea. The founder of this sporting event was an Irish actor and comedian called Thomas Doggett, who had a great enthusiasm both for the Sovereign, George I, and for the Thames Watermen; he also clearly had a flair for publicity.

On 1st August 1715 he affixed a placard on London Bridge which read: 'This being the (anniversary) day of His Majesty's happy accession to the throne there will be given by Mr Doggett an Orange Colour Livery with a Badge representing Liberty to be rowed for by Six Watermen that are out of their time within the year past. They are to row from London Bridge to Chelsea. It will be continued annually on the same day for ever.'

And so it has been. The race had to be cancelled during both World Wars, but the missed races were rowed consecutively in 1920 and 1947 respectively, to ensure that the continuity was not broken. It is sponsored by the Fishmongers' Company, of which Doggett was a member, and his portrait still hangs at their hall. The race is held in July, but with some changes since 1715. It is now rowed with the tide, not against it, and entry is open to all apprentices of the Watermen's Company, rather than to first-year men only. Also, to enable the winner to preserve his amateur status, a silver cup now replaces the financial rewards. The most coveted prize, however, is the coat (now red rather than orange) and the great silver badge, which the winner will wear on special occasions for the rest of his life.

On the day of the race, many launches assemble and the contest is started by the Bargemaster of the Fishmongers' Company, in his maroon uniform and cocked hat. Many former Doggett winners are present, and it is a memorable sporting and social occasion. It takes around twenty-five minutes to cover the course, and it is a true test of skill and endurance.

The winner receives his Coat and Badge at a special dinner in Fishmongers' Hall in November, when all former Doggetts attend and form a guard of honour for the new recruit.

The Royal Route

19. Buckingham Palace

Buckingham Palace is where most of London's ceremonial occasions originate. It is now thought of as the traditional royal residence in London, but it did not acquire that status until 1837, when Queen Victoria decided to make it her palace. It was originally built in 1704 as the London home of the Duke of Buckingham and was called Buckingham House. He sold it in 1762 to King George III, who wanted it as a dower house for Queen Charlotte, and it then became known as the Queen's House.

The Queen in the Gold State Coach on the celebration of the Golden Jubilee.

The Golden Jubilee of Her Majesty The Queen was celebrated in London on 3rd June 2002. There was a flypast by Concorde escorted by the Red Arrows, (above), and the crowd in The Mall (below) was estimated to have been one million strong..

George IV set about aggrandising it, employing John Nash as his architect, but he spent so much money that he nearly had to sell it. When the Houses of Parliament burned down in 1834, King William IV suggested that they might be replaced by Buckingham House. The problem was solved by Queen Victoria, who decided to make it London's Royal Palace.

As such, it is the scene of much ceremonial, in addition to the daily Changing of the Guard. All the Royal Processions in London start and end there, and the Royal Family also make their popular balcony appearances there on occasions such as Royal Weddings, Jubilees and The Queen's Birthday.

Much of London's ceremonial is planned there, for the Lord Chamberlain and his staff work in the Palace. It is also the scene of many royal events, such as some eleven **Investitures** every year, when The Queen personally presents honours and awards to about 130 people each time. Although it is not a public occasion, over 350 relatives and friends watch, and it is a scene full of splendour and tradition. It takes place in the Ballroom, and the Yeomen of the Guard are on duty, as well as two Gurkha Orderly Officers, as instituted by Queen Victoria.

The Ballroom is also the setting for **State Banquets**, which are a splendid scene, with a display of the magnificent royal gold and silver, and flowers and candles on the long tables, set for over 150 guests. Once again, the Yeomen are on duty, a reminder of the days when one of their duties was to serve some of the dishes and even to taste them to guard against any attempt to poison the Sovereign.

The gardens of Buckingham Palace are the scene for the three Royal Garden Parties that The Queen gives every year. Each one is attended by more than seven thousand guests from all over Britain and all walks of life.

Every summer The Queen opens Buckingham Palace to the public for several weeks, and it is possible to tour the State Apartments and see their many treasures.

19. The Royal Mews

Buckingham Palace may be the hub of London's ceremonial, but no State occasion can take place until the Crown Equerry has arranged for the Royal Mews to provide the necessary transport, whether coaches, carriages or cars. The present Royal Mews were originally the stables of Buckingham House and were redesigned in the 1820s by John Nash.

The fine collection of coaches and carriages kept there are for both ceremonial and everyday occasions. The showpiece is the incredibly ornate gold State Coach, built in 1762 for George III; it has been used for every Coronation since then and also for the Jubilees of 1977 and 2002. It is 24 feet (7.3 metres) long, weighs 4 tons and requires eight horses to pull it. Although it looks superb, it is not particularly comfortable. William IV said it was like a ship in a rough sea and George VI described his Coronation trip as 'one of the most uncomfortable rides I have ever had in my life'. But the suspension has been much improved since then.

Also on display are the Irish State Coach, used for the State Opening of Parliament, and the Glass Coach, which has been chosen for almost every Royal Wedding since it was acquired in 1911. There

The Gold State Coach.

A coach from the Royal Mews carries the Imperial State Crown to the State Opening of Parliament.

is also a collection of landaus, barouches and other carriages used on different State occasions.

The Queen's horses are also kept at the Royal Mews and the most famous are probably the Windsor Greys, which draw the State Coach. They are not a special breed but originate from the grey horses kept at Windsor in Victorian times, primarily for the driving carriages. They were moved to London just before the Second World War and have continued to be known as 'Windsor Greys'. They are strong, steady animals, at least 16.1 hands, and are named after places visited by The Queen.

The horses most in use today are probably the Bays, which are predominantly Cleveland Bays, supplemented by some from Holland, Germany and Ireland.

All the royal horses are given a very thorough training. They normally arrive aged about four and can then be expected to work for some fifteen years. In addition to learning to pull the carriages, they must above all be taught to remain calm in the face of traffic, bands, cheering crowds and camera flash-bulbs.

The Royal Grooms not only look after the horses and carriages, but may also be called upon to lead a procession as outriders, ride the carriage horses as postillions or drive as coachmen. They have four sets of uniform for different occasions. The grandest is Full State

Royal Grooms precede The Queen's coach through Horse Guards.

Dress, which is richly embroidered in gold and is so costly and difficult to replace that it is handed down from generation to generation. For lesser occasions there is Semi-State Dress, and Black is the everyday wear.

The horses too have different sets of harness for different occasions. There are eight sets of State harness altogether, all richly decorated with brass, except for the Number 1 State Harness, which has gilt ornaments; each weighs about 110 pounds (50 kg).

The Royal Mews are run by the Crown Equerry, who is responsible for organising all the royal transport on State occasions (and at any other time as well). It is an exacting task, where he must always be prepared for every possible contingency, however unlikely. Therefore, in the early hours of many mornings, carriage processions slip out of the Royal Mews to 'walk the course' with the Crown Equerry standing by, stop-watch in hand. Indeed, one dawn, a full eight months before The Queen's Silver Jubilee in 1977, the gold State Coach was drawn at a steady 3 mph (5 km/h) from the Royal Mews to St Paul's Cathedral and back, to check every timing to the nearest second. Such is the attention to detail that ensures the highest standards in all ceremonial.

21. Wellington Barracks

Wellington Barracks were built in 1834 and have been used by the Foot Guards ever since for their ceremonial duties. They were modernised in the 1980s but, happily, the original facade facing Birdcage Walk was preserved.

At about 11 a.m. every day, the New Queen's Guard can be seen forming up on the barrack square with the band playing. The Colour is brought on parade, and the Guard then marches off to Buckingham Palace.

After the Changing of the Guard, the Old Guard returns to Wellington Barracks to dismiss. It is worth following them and then visiting the **Guards Museum** which is located in Birdcage Walk, underground in front of the Guards Chapel at the Westminster end of the parade ground. It contains many interesting exhibits relating to the Guards in peace and war over three centuries, as well as videos of their ceremonial duties.

The Guards Chapel.

22. St James's Palace

On the north side of The Mall is St James's Palace, which became the Sovereign's main residence in 1689, when Whitehall Palace was burned down, and it then continued as such until 1837. It is still officially the seat of the Court, and foreign diplomats are accredited to 'The Court of St James'. It houses the Guard Room and the Officers' Mess of The Queen's Guard, and the Old Guard forms up there before marching to Buckingham Palace for the Changing of the Guard (see chapter 6). St James's Palace is also the home of the two oldest Royal Bodyguards in the world, the Yeomen of the Guard and the Gentlemen at Arms (see chapter 3).

Within the precincts of the Palace is the **Chapel Royal** where at Epiphany every year the ancient custom of presenting gold, frankincense and myrrh still continues. It dates back to medieval times, when the Sovereign made the offering in person. Today it is made on The Queen's behalf by two Gentlemen Ushers. It is an impressive ceremony, with the Yeomen of the Guard on parade, and a few tickets are available for the public.

Clarence House, which was the home of Queen Elizabeth The Queen Mother, is also within St James's Palace, and the Prince of Wales has his offices there too.

St James's Park was originally the royal garden to the Palace, and Charles II set up an aviary there, which has given its name to the present Birdcage Walk.

Between the Palace and the Park runs the magnificent, tree-lined ceremonial approach to Buckingham Palace, known as **The Mall**, running straight to Admiralty Arch. It is traditionally the prerogative of the Foot Guards to provide the street liners in The Mall on State occasions. The parts of the route further from Buckingham Palace are lined by the other Services.

23. Horse Guards

The Royal Route continues down The Mall to the **Horse Guards Parade**, originally a royal tiltyard for Whitehall Palace in Tudor times and still the largest clear space in London.

To the west on the edge of St James's Park is the **Guards Memorial**, a simple monument in white stone, which forms a dramatic backcloth to parades on Horse Guards. On the south side is Downing Street and to the east is the **Horse Guards Building**. This fine building dates from 1750 and was designed by William Kent and John Vardy. In the days before the Ministry of Defence it was the headquarters of the Commander-in-Chief of the British Army, and his office, overlooking the parade ground, is used as a vantage point by members of the Royal Family watching The Queen's Birthday Parade. Today it is the headquarters of the General Officer Commanding the Household Troops, who is responsible for organising almost all the military aspects of London's ceremonial. He sits at a desk once used by the Duke of Wellington when he was Commander-in-Chief from 1842 to 1852.

Also based there is the Silver Stick-in-Waiting, who commands the Household Cavalry and organises their ceremonial. His appointment dates back to the time of Charles II, who gave orders in 1678 that one of his Household Cavalry officers was to 'be in attendance on the King's person on foot, wheresoever he walk, from his rising to his going to bed', and that he should carry 'an ebony staff or truncheon with a gold head, engraved with His Majesty's cypher and crown'.

From this royal order date the offices of the Gold Stick-in-Waiting and the Silver Stick-in-Waiting. The latter is a serving officer, while Gold Stick is a senior retired officer who appears only on State occasions but then takes precedence over all other officers of the Armed Forces.

The Horse Guards Building also houses The Queen's Life Guard, as explained in chapter 5, and their guardroom and stables are there.

24. Whitehall

Opposite the Horse Guards Building is the **Banqueting House**, all that remains of Whitehall Palace, which was the home of the monarch from Tudor times until the reign of William and Mary. It is the work of the great architect Inigo Jones and is decorated with paintings by Peter Paul Rubens. It was on the balcony of the Palace that the execution took place on 30th January 1649 of King Charles I, who had walked there from St James's Palace, where he had taken communion in the Chapel Royal.

Just behind it is the **Ministry of Defence**, an unattractive building, but the scene of frequent Guards of Honour for visiting generals. This is an opportunity to see a hundred men of the Foot Guards marching with their band between Whitehall and Wellington Barracks, and The Queen's Life Guard turning out to them as they pass through Horse Guards Arch.

Almost opposite the Ministry of Defence is **Downing Street**, but there is no ceremonial to be seen there, only a solitary policeman outside Number Ten, the residence of the Prime Minister.

Further down Whitehall is the **Cenotaph**, scene of the solemn Remembrance Day Parade, described in chapter 16.

The Banqueting House in Whitehall.

25. Westminster Abbey

Westminster Abbey, or the Abbey Church of St Peter, Westminster, to give it its full title, has been closely connected with national ceremonial for nine centuries. It was built by King Edward the Confessor in 1065 for his personal use and today is a 'Royal Peculiar', that is a church whose allegiance is not to any bishop or archbishop, but directly to the Sovereign.

It has been used for Coronations ever since that of King Harold in January 1066, and the Coronation Chair is there. The only two Sovereigns who were not crowned in the Abbey were Edward V (1483) and Edward VIII (abdicated 1936).

The Abbey is also used for most Royal Weddings, though that of Prince Charles was an exception, being held at St Paul's Cathedral because the extra space available there was needed for the wedding of the Heir to the Throne. There were eleven Royal Weddings at the Abbey in the twentieth century.

For three centuries, from the time of Henry VIII onwards, all the Sovereigns were buried at Westminster Abbey, with three exceptions: Charles I, buried at Windsor in 1649; James II, buried at St Germain, France, in 1701; and George I, buried at Hanover, Germany, in 1727.

The west front of Westminster Abbey.

The Unknown Soldier's cortège passes the Cenotaph on 11th November 1920.

Then King George III built the Royal Vault at St George's Chapel, Windsor, and most Sovereigns since then have been buried there.

Someone else who is buried at Westminster Abbey is the **Unknown Soldier**, whose tomb of black marble lies just inside the West Door. He was interred with full military honours on 11th November 1920 at a ceremony attended by The King and many of the Royal Family, and there was a Guard of Honour of one hundred holders of the Victoria Cross. The idea was put forward originally by an Army chaplain, the Reverend David Railton MC, and the inscription on the tomb reads: 'They buried him among the Kings, because he had done good towards God and towards his House.' The Unknown Soldier's tomb is particularly honoured each year on Remembrance Sunday (see chapter 16).

Every third year or so the **Maundy Service** is held at Westminster Abbey; in the other years it is at cathedrals or abbeys outside London. The Queen attends and personally distributes the 'Royal Maundy', which consists of specially minted coins totalling as many pence as the Sovereign's years of age. It is presented to as many men and as many women as the Sovereign's age, a custom originated by King Henry IV (1399–1413).

The Maundy Service is a simple but deeply impressive occasion, when the Sovereign carries on a tradition that dates back to before the twelfth century. The Queen and all those officiating in the ceremony carry nosegays of spring flowers, with rosemary and thyme, a custom continuing from the times when they were used as a very necessary protection against the smells and infections of London's streets with their open drains.

The Yeomen of the Guard are in attendance as the 'Indoor Guard' and on their flat-topped hats three of them carry silver-gilt dishes, borrowed from the Tower of London for the occasion. The main dish, known as the Maundy Dish, was given by Charles II, while the others once formed part of the Royal Chapel plate. Further colour is added by the presence of the choir of the Chapel Royal at St James's Palace, who customarily attend the Maundy Service.

There are two distributions of Maundy gifts, each made personally by the Sovereign to every recipient. First, each of the women receives a green purse and each of the men a white purse containing £3.00, which is in lieu of what used to be a gift of clothing. At the second distribution each person is given two purses, one red and one white, with long strings attached. The red one contains £1.50 for provisions formerly in kind, and a payment of £1.00 as decreed by Queen Elizabeth I. The white purse contains the specially minted Maundy Money consisting of silver pennies (a coin dating back to AD 760), twopenny, threepenny and fourpenny pieces, which are legal tender but are seldom cashed and are nearly always kept as valued personal possessions.

Until 1951 the recipients of the Maundy alms used to be entitled to receive them every year but now that the service is held in a different place each year, they have one grant only. They used also to be chosen for their extreme poverty, but are now selected because of the service they have given to the Church and the community.

Also taking part in the ceremony are four Maundy Children, two boys and two girls. They represent the men who in earlier centuries attended the service girded with linen towels as a reminder to the congregation of the origin of the Maundy Service. The children no longer wear the towels, but they walk in the procession carrying the traditional nosegay and they receive a set of Maundy Money.

For the deserving men and women who receive their Maundy gifts from the Sovereign in person it is an unforgettable occasion.

Another ceremonial at Westminster Abbey is the **Installation Service for Knights Grand Cross of the Most Honourable Order of the Bath**. Every four years the service is held in the Henry VII Chapel, which is the chapel of the Order. It is usually attended by the Prince of Wales, who is the Grand Master, and he arrives at the Abbey in his impressive crimson mantle, wearing the insignia. It is a fine, colourful ceremony, as all the Knights Grand Cross in their mantles process through Westminster Abbey.

26. The Palace of Westminster

The original Palace of Westminster was the principal residence of the Sovereign from the time of Edward the Confessor (1042–66) until 1512, when a large part of it was burned down and Henry VIII decided to move to Whitehall Palace. In 1547 it assumed its present role as the seat of the two Houses of Parliament. Then on 16th October 1834 the whole Palace was destroyed by fire, with the exception of the magnificent Westminster Hall. In its place was erected a completely new building in the Tudor style. At one end is the world-famous clock-tower housing the bell, 'Big Ben', and at the other end the huge square Lords Tower. It was the creation of the architect Charles Barry and his collaborator, Augustus Welby Pugin, and survives today with little change. It covers 8 acres (3.2 ha), has 1100 rooms and a hundred staircases, but is still considered to lack adequate space for modern government.

The outstanding ceremonial at the Palace of Westminster is the State Opening of Parliament, described in chapter 14. Even though it is virtually impossible to obtain tickets for the ceremony, it is easy to

The King's Troop, Royal Horse Artillery, pull the gun carriage bearing the coffin of Queen Elizabeth The Queen Mother on the way to the Lying in State in Westminster Hall. This and the service in Westminster Abbey on 9th April 2002 were both most impressive and moving examples of London's ceremonial and traditions.

The coffin of Queen Elizabeth The Queen Mother, escorted by officers of the Regiments of which she was Colonel and by Guardsmen of the Irish Guards.

tour the Palace of Westminster and see where the ceremonial takes place: the House of Lords, the Royal Gallery, the Prince's Chamber and The Queen's Robing Room.

Westminster Hall is closely associated with national ceremonial and is the only part of the original palace to survive. Until 1882 it housed the four Courts of Justice and saw many famous trials, including those of Sir Thomas More in 1535, King Charles I in 1649 and Warren Hastings from 1788 to 1795. Oliver Cromwell was installed there as Lord Protector in 1653.

Today it is best known as the scene of the **Lying-in-State** of the Sovereign, of Queen Elizabeth The Queen Mother in 2002, and also of famous national figures such as Sir Winston Churchill. Formerly, the Monarch used to lie in state wherever he died. Henry VIII lay at Whitehall Palace and George III at Windsor, but since 1910 the formal Lying-in-State has been at Westminster Hall.

It is a worthy setting, 240 feet (73 metres) long and 68 feet (21 metres) wide. It was built by William Rufus in the 1090s, despite complaints that it was causing 'excessive taxes that never ceased'. Richard II added its unique hammerbeam roof three hundred years later.

A Lying-in-State is a most solemn and impressive sight. The catafalque stands in the centre of the hall, while members of the Royal Bodyguards keep continuous vigil. Nearest to the coffin stand four officers of the Foot Guards, since they are the Sovereign's Household Troops. Next are two officers of the Honourable Corps of Gentlemen-at-Arms, and then four Yeomen of the Guard.

The City of London

27. St Paul's Cathedral

St Paul's Cathedral, with its 365 foot (111 metre) dome rising above the City skyline, is the cathedral church of London. The present Renaissance masterpiece by Sir Christopher Wren was begun in 1675, the previous medieval building having been destroyed in the Great Fire of 1666.

It is an appropriate setting for many ceremonial occasions, and national **Thanksgiving Services** in particular have been held there for centuries. Queen Elizabeth I attended such a service on Sunday 27th November 1588 to give thanks for England's deliverance from the Spanish Armada. Nearly four centuries later Queen Elizabeth II did likewise after victory in the Falklands War of 1982.

St Paul's is also the scene for **State Funerals**. This is a rare honour reserved for outstanding national heroes, and there have been only three since the Cathedral was built. The first was Lord Nelson, whose body was brought by river from Greenwich, where it had been lying in state. After a State Funeral on 9th January 1806, it was laid to rest

The Duke of Wellington's tomb in the crypt of St Paul's.

Mounted Police lead the Funeral Procession of Lord Mountbatten across Horse Guards and past the Guards Memorial on the way to Westminster. Sailors are pulling the gun carriage on which the coffin rests.

in a vault placed directly under the centre of the dome of St Paul's.

When the Duke of Wellington died in 1852, Queen Victoria proposed that he should 'rest by the side of Nelson – the greatest military by the side of the greatest naval chief'. This was agreed and, after a most impressive funeral procession and service, the Iron Duke was interred alongside Nelson. His vast 17 ton tomb can still be seen in the crypt of St Paul's, where his and Nelson's bodies are the only ones interred there in their tombs rather than in the ground.

The only other State Funeral was that of Sir Winston Churchill in 1965, an occasion of stirring pageantry. The deeply moving service at St Paul's was followed by the unforgettable sight of his coffin being borne up the Thames on a launch for burial at Bladon, Oxfordshire. The Port of London Authority invoked the ancient custom of 'hushing' the river (ordering all movement and noise to cease) and the rows of riverside cranes dipped in an unofficial but historic salute to 'the greatest Englishman'.

One tomb not to be missed in St Paul's is that of Sir Christopher Wren himself. It bears the apt inscription *Si monumentum requiris, circumspice* ('If you seek his monument, look around').

St Paul's seems to be closely linked to funerals. The Great Bell there is tolled for two hours on the death of the Sovereign and for one hour when other members of the Royal Family die. It is also tolled on the death of the Archbishop of Canterbury, the Bishop of London, the Dean of St Paul's and the Lord Mayor, if they die in office. In the days before radio, the Lord Mayor was one of the first to be told of the Sovereign's death, so that he could order the Great Bell to be tolled and so pass on the news to the citizens of the capital. St Paul's, like Westminster Abbey, has links with the Orders of Chivalry. The Chapel of the Order of St Michael and St George and also of the Order of the British Empire are both within the cathedral, and services are held there once a year, with the officers and members of the Orders attending in their rich robes.

28. Guildhall

The heart of the City's ceremonial and traditions is Guildhall, standing within the sound of the famous Bow Bells, whose peals are said to have inspired Dick Whittington with the message 'Turn again, turn again, thrice Mayor of London'. The original building was badly damaged in the Great Fire of 1666 and again in the Blitz of 1940, but the fifteenth-century Great Hall, restored in the seventeenth century, is still largely intact.

Guildhall is used for meetings of the Corporation and of the Court of Aldermen, one of whose duties is to elect the Sheriffs and the Lord Mayor every year. It is the scene, too, of the installation of the new Lord Mayor at the ceremony of the Silent Change (see chapter 4).

It is best known perhaps for the **Banquets** that the Lord Mayor gives there, particularly the one on the first Monday of his term of office, when the Prime Minister traditionally attends and reports on government policies. It is a scene of great splendour, with trumpeters sounding fanfares, a band playing in the Musicians' Gallery, and the tables gleaming with silver and gold.

The highly valued honour of the **Freedom of the City** is also granted at a ceremony in Guildhall. It is normally obtained in one of three ways; by right of servitude, that is by apprenticement to a Freeman; by redemption, which is purchase with the approval of the Corporation; or by right of patrimony, that is to say by inheritance. It is also conferred on occasion by presentation, as a mark of distinction for exceptional services. King Charles II accepted the Freedom of the City in 1674, since when the names of many members of the Royal Family have appeared on the Roll of Freemen.

Prince Charles was granted the Freedom on 2nd March 1971, by patrimony through his father, who is a member of the Worshipful Company of Fishmongers. His Patrimony Voucher, which was 'in accordance with ancient custom' read aloud by the Principal Clerk to the Chamberlain, declared that 'His Highness Charles, Prince of Wales, Knight of the Most Noble Order of the Garter, is the son of His Royal Highness The Prince Philip, Duke of Edinburgh, Citizen and Fishmonger of London, and that He was born in lawful wedlock after the admission of His father into the Freedom of the City; and that He is His son so reputed and taken to be, and so they all say.' The Prime Warden and Wardens of the Worshipful Company of Fishmongers then formally presented Prince Charles to the Chamberlain, who, again 'according to ancient custom', addressed the Prince and presented him with a copy of his Freedom 'ornamentally written and emblazoned and sealed, in a suitable box'. Finally, the Lord Mayor

Gog, one of the two giant figures in Guildhall.

entertained his new Freeman to luncheon at the Mansion House.

Looking down on all this ceremonial from the Musicians' Gallery are the two legendary giants of the City of London, Gog and Magog, which have been part of the capital's traditions since the fifteenth century. For three hundred years they were made of wicker and carried in the Lord Mayor's Show. In Tudor times they were known as Gogmagog and Corineus, the former being an ancient inhabitant of Britain, armed with arrows and a globe of spikes, while the latter was a Trojan warrior in Roman costume with a spear and a shield. These names were too cumbersome and became shortened to Gog and Magog. The present wooden figures, 9 feet 3 inches (2.8 metres) tall, were carved to replace the previous 14 foot 6 inch (4.4 metre) figures, which dated back to 1708 but were destroyed in the Blitz, an event commemorated by a phoenix on Magog's shield.

29. The Tower of London

Nine centuries of history are embodied in the Royal Palace and Fortress of the Tower of London, and it is in effect the history of England. Kings and queens have been imprisoned, murdered and executed there, and, surprisingly perhaps, they also lived there quite happily until Elizabethan times.

The Tower has served not only as a fortress, prison and palace, but also as an Army barracks, the home of the Royal Mint for five hundred years (1344–1811), the first Royal Observatory and even a Royal Menagerie, with lions being housed there until one of them bit a sentry in 1835. Today it is the scene for the daily ceremonial of Guard Mounting and the unique Ceremony of the Keys (see chapters 7 and 8); in addition, Royal Salutes are fired there (see chapter 10), and there is much tradition behind the Installation of the Constable of the Tower and the ancient custom of Beating the Bounds. Looking after all this are the Yeoman Warders.

The Yeoman Warders

The present body of Yeoman Warders dates from 1485, but there have been warders at the Tower ever since it was built and they regard themselves with some justification as 'the oldest corps of men in the world still engaged in their original duties'.

With no captives to guard these days, they are mainly concerned to control and enlighten the many thousands of visitors to the Tower every day. They used until 1967 to look after the Crown Jewels, but these are now in the care of a separate body of curators and wardens.

A view of the Tower of London from across the river Thames.

A Yeoman Warder in semi-State Dress, without his ruff. He does not wear a cross-belt, as do the Yeomen of the Guard.

The Chief Yeoman Warder carries a Silver Mace, made in 1792 and surmounted by a silver model of the White Tower. Under him is the Yeoman Gaoler, who has a ceremonial axe.

This is not an executioner's axe but a ceremonial weapon dating back to Henry VII; it used to be carried in front of prisoners on their way by river from the Tower to and from Westminster, where they were tried. On the return journey, the positioning of the axe indicated the verdict; if the blade pointed towards the prisoner, he had been found guilty, and if it pointed away he was innocent.

The Yeoman Warders in State Dress carry a sword and an 8 foot (2.4 metre) halberd pike known as a partisan, but State Dress is worn only on the three Feast Days of Easter, Whitsun and Christmas, at the Installation of the Constable of the Tower and for Beating the Bounds. Everyday wear is a blue undress uniform approved by Queen Victoria in 1858.

In addition to looking after the many visitors to the Tower, the Yeoman Warders also care for the famous Tower ravens. A legend dating back to Charles II threatens that, when there are no longer any ravens in the Tower, both the White Tower and the Kingdom will collapse. Six birds are therefore carefully kept on the establishment, with a further two in reserve. Their wings are clipped and they are fed on a ration of eggs and horseflesh by the Yeoman Raven Master.

Installation of the Constable

The office of Constable of the Tower is one of the oldest in England, the first holder having been Geoffrey de Mandeville, a Norman knight who had distinguished himself at the Battle of Hastings in 1066. There have been over 150 since then, including eminent churchmen, politicians and soldiers. The office used to be held for life, and the Duke of Wellington was Constable for twenty-six years (1826–52), but in 1933 the tenure was limited to five years, and since 1826 the Constables have all been distinguished soldiers.

The Constable is installed at a short ceremony on Tower Green, with the Yeoman Warders and a band on parade, and a Guard of Honour, traditionally provided by his own regiment. The Lord Chamberlain, on behalf of the Sovereign, delivers to the Constable a set of keys and with them the custody of the Tower. The Constable replies: 'Lord Chamberlain, I accept the Keys and Custody of this Fortress which, in The Queen's name, you confide to my charge. As Constable, I will maintain Her Majesty's Tower, its rights and privileges against all comers.'

The Chief Yeoman Warder now doffs his headdress and cries 'God save Queen Elizabeth', to which all the Yeoman Warders respond 'Amen'. The keys are then given a Royal Salute before being handed over to the Lieutenant of the Tower.

The new Constable inspects the Yeoman Warders and then accompanies the Lord Chamberlain to the Queen's House, which is the residence within the Tower of the Resident Governor, who is also Keeper of the Jewel House, and the person responsible for looking after the Crown Jewels and the Tower.

Beating the Bounds

Every three years, on Ascension Day, a party of children associated with the Tower 'beats the bounds' of the Tower Liberty. This custom is of Saxon origin and was a means of recording boundaries in the days when they were often marked only by stones.

The ceremony begins with a short service in the chapel, after which the children are each issued with a willow wand and set out in procession on a tour of the twenty-nine boundary stones still in existence. Accompanying them are a detachment of Yeoman Warders in State Dress and also the Chaplain of the Tower, who declares, as they reach each stone, 'Cursed be he who removeth his neighbour's landmark'. The Chief Warder, who is also there, then gives the splendid order 'Whack it, boys, whack it', which they duly do.

All the bounds having been properly beaten, the party returns to the Tower, the National Anthem is sung, and the boundaries of the Tower are considered to be secure for another three years.

The Jewel House

A visit to the Jewel House is very much part of discovering London's ceremonial, for there you can see not only the Crown Jewels but also many other items connected with the pageantry of Britain. The Great Sword of State is there, which is carried before the Sovereign at a Coronation and at the State Opening of Parliament. There are Coronation Robes and the robes and insignia of the various Orders of Chivalry.

Most of the Crown Jewels date back only to the seventeenth century, for Oliver Cromwell ordered the destruction of all the treasures of the monarchy when he took power in 1650. He even broke up the Saxon crown of Edward the Confessor that had been used at Coronations for almost four hundred years. Only three items escaped: the Anointing Spoon, the Ampulla (a golden eagle holding the holy oil), and Queen Elizabeth's Salt. All three pieces are now on display.

All the remaining Crown Jewels had to be created again for the Coronation of King Charles II in 1661. A new St Edward's Crown was made for the occasion, but it is so heavy (weighing nearly 5 pounds or 2.3 kg) that it is only used for the actual Coronation and is then replaced by the lighter Crown of State, which was made for Queen Victoria and has been used at every Coronation since. Another beautiful crown is that made for the crowning of Queen Elizabeth (later The Queen Mother) in 1937, incorporating the famous Koh-i-noor Diamond.

30. The Future

Some cynics question whether there can be a future for ceremonial in the twenty-first century, but there can be little doubt that it will not only survive but continue to flourish, as it has done for a thousand years. Television is an important factor: before the Second World War, only those taking part and the patient crowds lining the streets saw much of State occasions, whereas today virtually the whole nation can watch them. In doing so, everyone participates to some extent and their emotions are stirred by what they see: sadness at the Remembrance Day Service, pride in the splendours of a Coronation or a Jubilee, and joy at a Royal Wedding.

It is a constant challenge to ensure that ceremonial adapts as necessary, but it has always done so successfully until now and will doubtless continue to do so. The judgement of those responsible will be as sure in the future as it has been in the past. But the overriding factor, is perhaps that the vast majority of the British people value their ceremonial and traditions as part of their national life, and as something to be appreciated and enjoyed.

Buckingham Palace during the Changing of the Guard ceremony.

Index

95